SUCCESS IN ANY ECONOMY

Copyright © 2023 CelebrityPress® LLC

All rights reserved. No part of this book may be used or reproduced in any manner whatsoever without prior written consent of the author, except as provided by the United States of America copyright law.

Published by CelebrityPress®, Orlando, FL.

CelebrityPress® is a registered trademark.

ISBN: 979-8-9862097-8-4
LCCN: 2023913173

This publication is designed to provide accurate and authoritative information with regard to the subject matter covered. It is sold with the understanding that the publisher is not engaged in rendering legal, accounting, or other professional advice. If legal advice or other expert assistance is required, the services of a competent professional should be sought. The opinions expressed by the authors in this book are not endorsed by CelebrityPress® and are the sole responsibility of the author rendering the opinion.

Most CelebrityPress® titles are available at special quantity discounts for bulk purchases for sales promotions, premiums, fundraising, and educational use. Special versions or book excerpts can also be created to fit specific needs.

For more information, please write:
CelebrityPress®
3415 W. Lake Mary Blvd. #9550370
Lake Mary, FL 32746
or call 1.877.261.4930

Visit us online at: www.CelebrityPressPublishing.com

SUCCESS IN ANY ECONOMY

CelebrityPress®
Lake Mary, Florida

CONTENTS

CHAPTER 1
PERFECT A GREAT SALES PROCESS
By Brian Tracy 9

CHAPTER 2
BUILDING AN ACCOUNTING ENTERPRISE
By James Thomasson 37

CHAPTER 3
THE POWER OF ATTITUDE, MOTIVATION, AND COMMITMENT IN BUSINESS SUCCESS
By Patrick Ziemer 47

CHAPTER 4
ESCAPE ARTIST
By Paul Herbka 57

CHAPTER 5
THE PITFALLS OF HIRING FRIENDS
By Dr. Heidi Gregory-Mina 67

CHAPTER 6
LIVING AND WORKING WITH TRUE AUTHENTICITY IN THE WORKPLACE
By James Radford 77

CHAPTER 7
BECOME FREE BY REPLACING YOURSELF
By Mike Heckman 89

CHAPTER 8
THE IMPOSSIBLE DREAMS
By Paul P. Phimasone 101

CHAPTER 9
BEYOND THE BOX
DISRUPT. IMPACT. INSPIRE.
By Bably Bhasin 111

CHAPTER 10
TO THRIVE IN A DOWN ECONOMY, YOU MUST BE...YOU!
By Shawn Mason 121

CHAPTER 11
NIDO'S LAWS FOR MAKING YOUR WAY THE WINNING WAY
By Nick Nanton 129

CHAPTER 1

PERFECT A GREAT SALES PROCESS

BY BRIAN TRACY

Nothing happens until a sale takes place.
~ Red Motley

Many businesses are started by people with no sales experience. They may be entrepreneurs who love a product, or invented one, and now they have to sell it. But they have no idea what goes on in the interaction between the careful, cautious, skeptical potential customer and salesperson. They think that sales fall from the sky, like the rain, if you have a good enough product or service. They are then astonished when their companies run out of customers, cash, and credit, and they go bankrupt. The adage, "If you build it, they will come," is rarely true. In business, 'they'—the customers—will come only if they want to.

In today's environment, any business that wants to successfully sell its products and services must begin by understanding exactly who its customers are and why they buy.

THE NEW REALITIES OF SELLING

There is more competition for every business than ever before, and the competition is getting stiffer every week and every month. Customers today are tougher to sell to than ever before. They are more demanding with regard to quality, service, and value. Customers today have more choices and therefore less urgency to decide. Customers are impatient; they want everything now.

WHAT CUSTOMERS WANT

In selling a great product or service, perhaps the most important word is consistency. Your customer must consistently enjoy the results that you promised – to induce the customer to buy your product in the first place. If your product delivers on its promises 90 percent of the time, then your quality rating is 90 percent. Your ultimate goal is to achieve a rating of 100 percent, which is the rating that you earn when your product or service consistently and dependably delivers on your promises 100 percent of the time. This is what causes customers to say you have a "great product!"

THREE TYPES OF CUSTOMERS

There are three types of customers to whom you might be selling:

- First, there are businesses that use your product or service in the course of their activities.
- Second, there are businesses that resell your product or service in the market.
- Third, there are consumers who buy and use your product or service to enhance their personal lives.

Each of these customers has a different set of needs to which you must appeal. All buying behavior, however, is aimed at the achievement of a definite *improvement* of some kind. The product or service must solve a problem, satisfy a need, or achieve a goal. To offer a great product or service, you must be absolutely clear about what your product or service is intended to accomplish for your customer.

The goal of any business is to serve its customers and generate a profit, to generate revenues in excess of costs. A business can accomplish profitability by selling more of its products and services, by selling them at a higher price, by achieving repeat business, or by lowering the costs involved in selling, producing, and delivering the product or service in the first place.

Selling Great Products to Business Customers

Decision makers responsible for business purchases think continually about the bottom line, about how your product or service will affect net profits. In the simplest terms, in selling to a business, your primary aim must be to demonstrate that your product or service will generate greater efficiency, effectiveness, and therefore more bottom-line income or savings than the amount the customer will pay for what you sell.

Ideally, in selling to businesses, your job is to convince the decision maker that your product is, whenever possible, actually 'free, plus a profit.' In other words, your product contributes to your customer's bottom line and it makes them more profitable and successful than they would have been without it.

Your job is to demonstrate that, if the business purchases your product or service, the benefit that it can expect in net dollar terms will be well in excess of the cost. If your product costs $100,000 and saves or makes the business customer $50,000 per year, and continues to perform effectively for five years, the customer will get a 50 percent return on his money each year for two years, and then a net of $50,000 to the bottom line for the next three years. In this case, your product or service is 'free, plus a profit.'

Of course, there are many products and services that businesses buy to satisfy ego or aesthetic desires. But even a product or service designed to improve the attractiveness or beauty of a business office or a location is ultimately aimed at attracting and keeping more customers and making more profitable sales.

Business customers want answers to four questions before committing to buying a product or service:

1. What is the value equation? (relative cost, quality, reliability)
2. How much do I get back? (return on investment, assets, clients)
3. How soon do I get it back, or on what schedule? (time to pay back)
4. How sure can I be that I will actually enjoy the bottom-line financial benefits that you are offering? (risk management and guarantee issues)

These questions are usually unspoken, but they exist in the mind of the buyer. If you fail to answer them satisfactorily in the course of your sales presentation, the customer will put off the buying decision, or not buy at all. The single most important determinant of whether a business buys your product or service and considers it to be a high-quality offering is *time to pay back*. The sooner your product or service pays for itself and begins yielding a net financial benefit to your customer, the faster and easier it is for the customer to purchase your product or service. Your ability to demonstrate rapid payback and to convince the customer that he will enjoy this result with a high degree of certainty is central to your making the sale in the first place.

Selling Great Products to Wholesalers or Retailers

The motivation of this second type of customer is very different from the business customer. The primary concern of the retailer is net profit as the result of either high turnover or high profitability per unit sold, or both.

Of course, retailers want their customers to be happy. For this reason, they will be demanding high quality in the product you offer and requiring that you guarantee absolute satisfaction to their customers.

At one time, you had to offer an excellent product or service—

one that delivered on your promises consistently—in order to increase sales, market share, and profitability. But today, your product or service must be excellent for you to even enter into a competitive market. Wholesalers and retailers have a lot of choices when it comes to products they will carry and services they will offer.

Selling Great Products to Consumers

The third type of customer that you sell to will be the consumer. The consumer or end user of your product or service has different motivations from the business customer or other resellers. Consumers seek improvement in their life or work. The consumer is more concerned about what your product or service 'does" rather than what it 'is.'

Customers are emotional. Their primary motivation to purchase what you sell is their anticipation of how they will feel after having bought from you. Will they feel happy? Proud? Secure? More attractive? More respected? Richer? More confident?

There is a difference between consumer needs and wants. They are not the same. People may *need* to be healthy, thin, and fit, but they *want* to eat delicious foods in large quantities. A product or service that seems like a logical choice may not be an emotional preference. Your ability to separate these issues is essential for your success in triggering the desired consumer response.

What do consumers really want? When grocers such as Whole Foods Market promoted the personal health benefits and enhanced environmental impact of organic foods, it wasn't enough. For consumers to pay more, the food had to taste much better, too. When consumers discovered that organic ingredients made fancy cuisine taste great, a multibillion-dollar industry sprang out of the commodity grocery business.

When you go to a restaurant and order a meal, you want to be able to say afterward, that "This is a great restaurant." The goal of the restauranteur and every person who interacts with the dining customer must be aimed at triggering this response.

To offer any great product or service, you must be absolutely clear about the feeling that your product or service will create for your potential customer. It is only when you can generate that feeling and deliver on your promise that customers will call it a 'great' product.

THREE WAYS TO INCREASE SALES

There are basically three ways to increase sales:

1. **Increase the number of transactions**. Volume can be accomplished through marketing and advertising, using special promotions, discounts, and a variety of other means to get customers to buy from you for the first time.

2. **Expand the size of each transaction**. Once you have attracted a prospect, you can up-sell, cross-sell, and even down-sell if the customer cannot afford the main product or service.

3. **Increase the frequency of purchases**. You can take such good care of the customer that she buys again and again. This is obviously the most efficient type of customer interaction—selling more to existing buyers. All good business is about 'exceeding customer expectations.' The key measure of customer satisfaction is repeat business. It is not possible for a business to succeed in the long term unless it takes such good care of its customers that they return again and again. This is only possible when the business can trigger the response: "This is a great product!"

SET YOUR OWN BAR

Your competitors wake up every morning thinking about how

to get your customers, take your business away from you, and put you out of business, if possible. Your competitors are often obsessed with winning your customers' attention. Just like you, they realize that there is fierce competition for customer dollars, and they are determined to get as many of them as possible, even if that means that you get none at all. The best salespeople are obsessive about follow-up and the relentless pursuit of the best prospects.

Your job is to learn everything you possibly can about your competitors so that you can assess their strengths and weaknesses in the marketplace, then set your own bar. With more and more salespeople descending on fewer and fewer customers, persistence and knowledge matter more than ever before.

In *Blue Ocean Strategy: How to Create Uncontested Market Space and Make Competition Irrelevant*, W. Chan Kim and Renée Mauborgne encourage you to set your own buying criteria for your business rather than rely on your competitors to determine quality, price, and ultimately, the survival of your products and services. They argue that you can sidestep 'red oceans' of competition by not following their lead, by redefining a market and setting your own new rules.

Their favorite example is Cirque du Soleil, a company that created an entirely new way for people to think about the circus and, in turn, resuscitated a dying industry. It was a brilliant and fresh way to recapture entertainment dollars and it caught competitors flat-footed. Cirque du Soleil redefined the rules and reinvented the customer experience, and its new style of entertainment product sold itself.

THE MEASURE OF SALES SUCCESS

Customer retention is the key to sales success. Single-purchase customers are too hard and expensive to acquire. Your focus must be on the second sale, and the third sale. Your goal must be resales to the same customer, over and over. In addition, your goal should be to get referrals from your satisfied customers.

The most important sale is not the first sale; it is the *second*.

You can win the first sale with promises, special offers, and discounts, but you only attract repeat business when your customers feel that you delivered on your promises. This causes them to prefer to buy from you again rather than someone else.

The second sale takes approximately one-tenth of the time and expense to attract, and it is therefore much easier and more profitable than the first sale. The fact is that winning customer loyalty today is harder than ever before. It takes more calls to find qualified prospects. It takes more callbacks to make individual sales, or more contacts or visits. It takes more service. This is why the majority of sales, and the largest purchases, from the most successful retailers and wholesalers, come from repeat customers, not from first-time buyers.

The way that you generate repeat business is with high-quality products and outstanding customer service. The true measure of the success of your business is the percentage of your business that comes from repeat sales and referrals.

WHERE THE RUBBER MEETS THE ROAD

Your ability to actually *sell* the product, to convert the interested prospect into a confirmed customer, is where the rubber meets the road. It is another critical determinant of business success. Your ability to sell effectively flows from everything we have talked about in this program up until now.

Fortunately, all sales skills are learnable. You can learn any sales skill you need to learn to accomplish any sales goal you can set for yourself or for your business. There are no limits.

PERFECT A GREAT SALES PROCESS

Selling is a simple, practical, proven process that has been learned and relearned hundreds of thousands of times by individuals and organizations. It can be learned and practiced by you so that your customers will say afterward: "This has been a great buying experience!"

When I started out in sales, I had no idea what I was doing. After working at laboring jobs for several years, and with no high school diploma, I got a job in straight commission sales, knocking on doors, cold-calling from dawn to dusk. I would start at 7:30 or 8:00 a.m., when people arrived at work, call on businesses all day, and then go out into the neighborhoods, calling on homes and apartments in the evenings. The only good news was that I was not afraid to work. I just wasn't making any sales.

After six months of fourteen-hour days, six days a week, barely making enough money to pay for one room in a small boarding house, I realized that a desire to be successful wasn't enough. I could barely sell anything. Finally, I did something that changed my life. I went to the most successful salesman in the company and asked him what he was doing differently from me that enabled him to sell five and ten times as much as anyone else.

He took me aside and went over my sales process with me and showed me how to sell professionally. He told me the correct sequence of steps in a sales presentation, the questions to ask, and how to answer objections. He told me how to ask for the sale, and how to get referrals. And I did what he told me.

And my sales went up, and up, and up!

What I learned, and what I subsequently relearned over the course of my business life, is that if you do what other successful people do, nothing can stop you from eventually getting the same results that they do. If you sell like other successful salespeople and companies sell, you will soon get the same results that they do. And if you don't, you won't.

A DOCTOR OF SELLING

Salespeople at every level should view themselves as 'doctors of selling.' This is a helpful model that is easy to teach and easy to learn. If you go to a doctor of any kind, anywhere in the world, the doctor always follows an established procedure. It consists of three steps: examination, diagnosis, and recommended treatment or prescription. Salespeople should follow the same three-step model in their sales activities.

(a) The Examination

Just as a doctor would insist upon doing a complete examination of the patient before drawing any conclusions or making any recommendations, you must do the same thing with each prospect.

Never assume that one size fits all. Never conclude that the reason someone bought your product or service is identical to the reason that another person might buy your product or service. Before a great salesperson launches into a presentation, they listen to the customer carefully.

During the information-gathering process, discipline yourself to hold back from talking about your product or service or making recommendations. A doctor would not start talking happily away about various pills that he might prescribe for a particular ailment before he had finished examining you. So, be patient. Ask a lot of questions. Do a thorough examination of the needs, wants, hopes, and desires of the customer.

(b) The Diagnosis

In this stage, you take all of the information that the customer has given you and double-check it for accuracy by asking questions to test your understanding. You then share with the prospect what you believe his real want or need is, and how it could be satisfied.

Many patients do not have a clear understanding about their real problem or needs. This is why a good doctor will always explain his findings to you, explain the various courses of treatment available to you, and then recommend what might be the best treatment for you personally.

It is the physician's job, like the salesperson, to educate the patient about the various possibilities available. This process gives you credibility as a knowledgeable source of information and makes it clear that you have empathy for the customer's challenges. It opens the customer to listen to the range of solutions you are selling.

(c) The Prescription

Only after you have done a thorough examination, and both discussed and agreed upon the diagnosis with the prospect, do you move to the third phase: the prescription or course of treatment. This is where you recommend the ideal product or service for this prospect, all things considered, and urge the prospect to take action.

A great insulation salesperson doesn't just show up to sell top-quality products and offer excellent prices. They first examine your house to understand how it is built and to find out how much you are currently paying in energy costs. They then show you how you are spending twice as much as your neighbor on your energy bills because you have older insulation. They tell you about how your neighbors have fewer allergy symptoms because they don't have mildew in the attic from old insulation. They explain why your neighbor's house smells cleaner and fresher. They then recommend a course of action that you can take to install better insulation and get all the benefits that you have told them that you want.

Salespeople should consider themselves doctors of selling, as complete professionals who practice a craft, operate with a code of ethics, follow a set of procedures that work, and are completely devoted to the well-being of the customer (patient). This attitude of professionalism is practiced by the top 20 percent of sales professionals in every field.

SEVEN RULES FOR A GREAT SALES PROCESS

Professional selling is an art and science, like cooking. Don't go into the kitchen without the following *seven* sacred ingredients. If you are lacking any one for your recipe, or if you mix them in the wrong order or proportion, the sale will not take place.

If you prefer, here's another analogy: Selling is like dialing a seven-digit telephone number. You must press each number in the proper sequence if you want to get through to the person at the other end of the line. In selling, you must follow this specific seven-step sales process to ensure the maximum number of sales, resales, and referrals.

Rule 1: Prospects versus Suspects

The first rule for sales success is 'spend more time with better prospects.' There may be many prospects for what you sell, but they are not all *your* prospects. We are cautioning you here about your sales process. Most prospects are inappropriate for your company and your products and services. Who are the primary buyers of your product or service? In most businesses, it is likely that less than 20 percent of your customers buy 80 percent of what you sell. You have to make it your business to find those customers who are in the top 20 percent. If you are a discount stockbroker, you have to find the customers who trade the most. If you sell advertising, you have to find the clients who buy the most advertising.

It sounds obvious, but many business owners behave as if they have no idea who their best customers are. We are amazed at how often we go into companies where they have done extensive research in the marketing department, but nevertheless, the sales group ends up wasting time and money shooting in all directions. Get your customer service people and your marketing team and your sales force all together to talk about the best buyers in your market.

Your first job is to separate prospects from 'suspects.' Take your time and ask questions. Your sales energies and resources are limited. You cannot waste them by spending too much time with people who either cannot or will not buy. A good prospect has qualities that fall into several categories:

- **Timing**. The prospect has a genuine need that your product or service can satisfy, and he has that need now.
- **Problem**. The prospect has a clear, identifiable problem that your product or service can solve.
- **Value**. The prospect has a clear goal of what your product or service will help them to achieve at a cost that is clearly less than the value of the goal itself.
- **Pain**. Your prospect is dissatisfied or has discontent of some kind that your product or service can take away.
- **Result**. The prospect has a definite result that they want and need to accomplish, and your product or service will help them to achieve that result faster, better, and cheaper than they could in the absence of what you are selling.

In every case, the most important factor is clarity. Both you and the prospect need to be completely clear that the need, problem, goal, result, or pain exists and that your product or service is a cost-effective way of dealing with it.

Rule 2: Establishing Rapport and Trust

Despite all the data and expertise invested in the sales process, the vast majority of buying decisions end up being made on the basis of *emotion*, especially about how buyers (or their peers) feel about the product and the salesperson. How buyers feel about the salesperson extends to how they feel about the entire company.

The best sales process is one in which you educate consumers about the problems they face—with great factual detail—and then demonstrate the benefits provided by the solutions you are selling. However, the biggest part of the sale goes on after the sale. Once you have made the sale, you must deliver the product or service, make sure that it is satisfactorily installed and utilized, and take care of customer concerns or complaints for a substantial time afterward. That is why the customer wants a relationship first. As far as the customer is concerned, the relationship with the salesperson can become more important than the product or service you are selling. There is a 'law of indirect effort' in selling. It says that the more you focus on the relationship (the indirect approach), the more the sale will take care of itself. But the more you focus on the sale, ignoring the relationship, the less likely it is that you will achieve either a sale or a good customer relationship.

The most important elements in a sales relationship are trust and credibility. The customer must trust you (the salesperson) completely and have complete confidence that you will fulfill your promises. The customer must believe that your product or service will do what you say it will do and continue doing it.

Telling is not selling. There is a direct relationship between the number of questions you ask about the customer's wants and needs, and the strength of the relationship that you form. Telling is not selling. Only asking is selling.

In addition, there is a direct relationship between how carefully you listen to the customer's answers, and how much the customer likes and trusts you. The fact is that *listening builds trust*. There is no faster or more effective way to build a high-trust relationship between the salesperson and the customer than for the salesperson to ask lots of questions and listen carefully to the answers.

The more closely you listen to the customer when they speak, the more they will like and trust you and be open to buying your product or service. Questions are the key and trust is the essential factor.

Rule 3: Identifying Needs Accurately

Many customers do not know that they have a need that your product or service can satisfy when they first talk to you. In their minds, they are tire kickers; that is, they are simply gathering information.

When you speak to a customer, they may have a need that is *clear, unclear, or nonexistent.* If the need is clear, the customer may be accurate or inaccurate about how to satisfy that need. Maybe what they need is very different from what they think they need.

If the need is unclear, it is only through the examination and diagnosis process that you and the customer become clear on exactly what need exists and how it can best be satisfied with what you offer.

In many cases, the customer may think that they have a need, but their situation is really satisfactory as it is. They do not need your product or service, and it is your duty as a professional to tell them that.

The way you identify needs accurately is by asking questions, from the general to the particular, and listening to the answers. This is why the highest-paid salespeople prepare their questions carefully in advance, writing them down, and asking them in sequence.

The worst salespeople say whatever falls out of their mouths and lurch back and forth through the sales conversation like a drunk staggering from lamppost to lamppost. A disjointed questioning process invariably lowers credibility and makes the sale increasingly difficult to achieve.

Rule 4: Presenting Persuasively

The presentation is where the actual sale is made. You can make a lot of mistakes in the sales process, but the quality of your presentation determines whether or not the customer buys.

The best sales method is to *show, tell, and ask a question*. For example, you say: "This is a small business accounting software program. With it, you can manage all the numbers in your business. Is this something that would be of interest to you?" Use the 'trial close' throughout your presentation. This is a closing question that can be answered with a 'no' without stopping the sales process because it allows the salesperson another opportunity to respond. For example:

Salesperson: Would you want to install this software on your home office computer?

Customer: No. I would rather use it in my office downtown.

Salesperson: No problem. It works equally well on either home computer or server operating systems.

In addition, a powerful and professional sales presentation is one that continually refers to other customers who have used the product or service successfully in the past. Tell stories about other customers who are in the same or a similar situation as this prospect, but who bought the product or service and were happy as a result.

Rule 5: Answering Objections Effectively

There are no sales without objections. Objections indicate interest. The more the prospect questions you about your product or service, the more likely it is that she is interested enough to buy it.

The 'law of six' applies to objections. It says that there are never more than six objections to any product or service offering.

Sometimes there are only one or two, but never more than six. Your job is to sit down with a sheet of paper and write out the answer to the question: *What are all the reasons that a qualified prospect might give me for not buying my product or service?*

Even if you receive dozens of objections in the course of a week or a month, they can all be clustered around no more than six categories. Your job is to identify the major objections that you are likely to get and then to develop bulletproof, logical answers to each of those objections so that they do not stop the sales process.

Rule 6: Closing the Sale

In golf, they say, "You drive for show, but you putt for dough." In sales, you follow every step we have talked about up until now, but your ability to close the sale and to get the prospect to make a buying decision is where you 'putt for dough.'

The most powerful word in the sales process is 'ask.' Most people are terrified of rejection, of being told 'no' in a sales conversation. For this reason, they don't ask at all. They sit there passively and hope the customer will take the initiative and buy their product or service. But this seldom happens. Even if the customer wants the product, needs it, can use it, and can afford it, the responsibility of the salesperson is to reach out verbally and ask for a buying decision.

Making an invitational close. Perhaps the simplest of all closing techniques is the *invitational close*. After you have made a presentation, you ask: "Do you have any questions or concerns that I haven't covered so far?"

When the customer says, "No, I think you've covered everything," you then roll into an invitational close by saying, "Well, then, why don't you give it a try?"

Alternatively, you could talk about how they would like the

product or service delivered. Many customers are only one question away from buying. All they need is a little nudge or encouragement. When you ask, "If you like it, why don't you give it a try?" you will be amazed at how many people say, "Sure, why not?"

The good news is that if you have built a high level of rapport and trust, identified needs accurately, made a clear benefit-oriented presentation, and answered any objections the prospect has, the closing of the sale follows naturally. It is simple and easy and almost foreordained. You must never be afraid to ask.

Rule 7: Getting Resales and Referrals

This is the most important part of the sales process. Everything must be aimed at taking such good care of your customer that they buy from you again and recommend you to their friends and associates. Treat them like a *million-dollar customer*, as if they had the ability to purchase enormous quantities of your product and to recommend you to a substantial number of other prospects.

On average, a person knows 300 people by their first names. They can be friends, relatives, teachers and classmates, coworkers or other job-related contacts, and associates of all kinds, such as your banker or accountant.

Imagine that only 10 percent of the people whom one of your customers knows are prospective customers for your products or services as well. This would mean that each person who buys from you has the potential to bring you *thirty* additional customers if you treat your current customer really well. Each of those thirty additional customers also knows 300 people. And approximately 10 percent of those additional people can buy from you as well.

This means that each person that you sell to can potentially bring you 900 (30 x 30) prospects in the months ahead. Does that get your attention? Does that have an effect on the way you treat the individual customer standing in front of you? We hope so.

Selling to a referral takes one-fifteenth of the time, money, and energy required to sell to a cold call or a new customer. In consumer retailing, for example, when someone is referred to you by a happy customer, that person is 95 percent sold before they've even contacted you for the first time. Word-of-mouth is extraordinarily powerful in growing your business if you can tap into it on a regular and systematic basis.

Asking for referrals. The key to getting referrals is to 'be referable.' Give such good service and educational information to the customer that they feel confident recommending you to their friends, family, and associates. When you take good care of your customers, they will want their friends to enjoy the same experience.

Be sure to ask for referrals at every opportunity. You can say, "Mr. Prospect, I really like working with people like you. Do you know any other great people like yourself who might be interested in my product or service?"

Who is going to tell you that they don't know any other *great people*?

When you get a referral from a happy customer to a new prospect, be sure to report back to the customer and share exactly what happened. People are inordinately curious about what you did and said to their friends or associates, and how they responded.

When you make a sale to a referral, send a thank-you letter or, even better, a gift to the source of the referral. My favorite choice is a gift basket with delicious foods of some kind. People always like to receive gifts, and they will be much more likely to give you more referrals in the future if you show your appreciation.

There are many books, articles, CDs, and sales training programs that expand on these seven steps in the sales process. What's especially important to know is that sometimes, a small improvement in any one area can lead to a dramatic improvement in your success.

SIX ELEMENTS OF MEGA-CREDIBILITY IN SELLING

Today, it takes credibility for you to get a hearing with a prospect, but it takes mega-credibility for you to get the sale. There are six elements of mega-credibility you can develop and use in your sales activities:

1. Your market visibility
2. Your company
3. Testimonials
4. Professional presentation
5. Your salesperson
6. The product itself

Your Visibility in the Market

Few things are more effective in building credibility than to be a 'known quantity' in your business. The best sales organizations are intimately tied into the activities of the press organizations that specialize in their industry. They know the top reporters and editors. They make presentations at all the key trade shows. They become valued volunteer officers of the right professional associations. They participate in their professional service organizations and the community organizations that give them visibility. They know the analysts who write research reports, the columnists who specialize in their industry, and the bloggers who cover their market. They write their own blogs and newsletters, helping to educate customers in the marketplace.

Who are the people who 'influence' your clients most? Who are the thought leaders they look to for advice and insights? What publications and/or thought leaders do your prospects pay the most attention to? Who has the most impact on public opinion about your product or service?

Your Company

Your company has three elements that build credibility: its *size*, *reputation*, and *longevity*. With regard to size, the bigger a company is, the more it is assumed to be offering a high-quality product or service. Why else would so many people buy so much of it?

If you don't have size going for you, then you need to compensate with other creative and useful features that make your offering better. As a small businessperson, you must demonstrate that big is not always better—your small business provides more specialized or more personal and attentive service, for instance.

The longevity of your company could make its products more trustworthy. There is a natural assumption that if your company is large, has a good reputation, and has been in business for a long time, it must be selling high-quality products and services that are obviously worth more than those sold by newer or lesser-known companies.

The reputation of a company is extremely important, perhaps more than any other factor, in building mega-credibility. One of the most powerful trust-building actions a salesperson can take is to mention how large the company is and how respected it is in the industry. Never assume that your prospective customers have any knowledge about your company when they first talk to you.

Testimonials

Testimonials are a great way to demonstrate and promote your reputation in the market with your prospects. After all, one of the most common, though sometimes unspoken questions that every customer has is: "Who else has bought your product or service?"

There is nothing that builds the credibility of a product, service, or company faster than the knowledge that lots of people, hundreds or thousands, have already bought the product or service, with satisfactory results.

Be sure to tell the prospect how many people have already bought this product or service and are currently enjoying it. Share with the prospective customer testimonial letters from your existing customers. Show the customer lists of other people who have bought the product or service. Show the customer photographs of other customers using or enjoying the product or service you are selling. Shoot video testimonials from happy customers and play them for your prospect on your laptop.

The use of testimonials is one of the fastest and most powerful ways to build the mega-credibility you need to make the sale.

Professional Presentation

Your sales presentation must be thorough, prepared, and customized for this prospect. By some estimates, you can increase the perceived value of a product or service by two or three times by the simple act of presenting it professionally. That means doing careful preparation in advance and learning everything you can about the customer. You plan your presentation thoroughly, in every detail. You make your presentation smoothly and fluently, answering each of the customer's questions or concerns. A professional sales presentation—customized for your specific client's needs and challenges—significantly lowers fear and skepticism and raises trust and credibility.

Your Salesperson

The quality, character, and confidence of the salesperson have a huge influence on the sales result, and they are conveyed, variously, by the salesperson's conduct and appearance, knowledge, and attitude.

- **Conduct and Appearance.** It's difficult to build a relationship with your customers if they are uncomfortable with you from the moment you meet them. Do you know how to behave appropriately with your prospects? Do you speak your customer's language? Do you understand their culture and customs? Do you dress for success so that you are taken seriously in the customer's organization?

  It is absolutely essential that salespeople study proper conduct, behavior, and dress for the business, organization, or individual to whom they are selling. The rule is, "If it doesn't help, it hurts." Everything counts.

- **Knowledge.** The best salespeople learn every possible detail they can about the customer's business before they meet with the customer for the first time. They research and think through how the customer can most benefit from what they are selling. The more you can demonstrate genuine interest and value-added knowledge about how the product or service will be used, the more powerful an impact you will have on the prospect.

  While there is much truth to the notion that a talented salesperson can 'sell anything' to anyone, the greatest salespeople generally care enough about the customer and the product to become an expert. They are genuinely concerned about their customers and want to help them to solve their problems and achieve their goals.

- **Attitude.** Top salespeople love and enjoy the products they sell. They like to talk about it and explain it to others, especially customers. They want to learn more about their product and what it can do for their customers. People who love their work and think it matters will learn twice as much and work twice as hard as those who don't.

Authenticity or Arrogance?

Many people try to express their individuality by using humor or gestures, or by dressing or grooming themselves in a way that draws attention to them. While you might sincerely be trying to be authentic and to 'be yourself' (and your heart is in the right place), customers or their organizational culture may not appreciate it. They may not understand your intentions. They may see your lack of sensitivity to their sensibilities as arrogance, or worse.

It is arrogant not to do your homework first. You need to show respect in a way that doesn't compromise who you are. That means understanding everything you can about the world your customer lives in.

For guidance on proper appearance and conduct, study the most successful salespeople in your field. They are not all the same either in terms of background, temperament, or personality. How are they reaching out to prospects in ways that honestly win the trust of their customers? Follow their lead; harvest their insights. Get in step with your customer.

The Product Itself

The final element for building mega-credibility is an ability to demonstrate to the customer that your product or service is the ideal one for him at this time, and that your price is reasonable and fair, relative to the value that the customer receives. Having the right product for the right customer at the right time and at the right price is the ultimate test of credibility.

The Three P's of High Performance

In our research for *Success Built to Last*, we studied people who were high achievers for at least twenty years—from billionaires to Nobel Laureates. Despite their field or profession, we found they have three traits in common that are difficult for a leader to fake: *passion, purpose,* and *performance.* They love what they do (passion) and think that it is important to customers (purpose). When they are clear about their passion and purpose, they become intensely result and action-oriented (performance). When all three traits are combined in your sales work, you'll win sales time after time. When you take the time to learn about your customers' passions, purpose, and performance, you will bond with them. Customers will enjoy being with you and feel confident buying from you.

THE ULTIMATE TEST

In the final analysis, your ability to convert interested prospects into buying customers is the critical measure that determines success or failure. Top companies of all sizes see themselves as 'sales organizations.' The top people think about customers and sales all day long. The best salespeople are the highest paid and most respected people in the organization.

In sales, remember that *you become successful when you give success to others.* If your financial results are not what you want today, put everything else aside and get out there and talk to buyers. Partner with your customers and commit to helping them achieve their goals. Sell something you really believe in that provides lasting value to customers, and they'll reward you by sending money right back in your door. And never give up!

CHECKLIST FOR PERFECTING A GREAT SALES PROCESS

1. Identify the three most important **factors that influence and determine the success** of salespeople in your company or industry.
   a. _____
   b. _____
   c. _____

2. List three actions you could take immediately to **attract more and better prospects** to your business.
   a. _____
   b. _____
   c. _____

3. What are the three most important **sales skills** that you and your salespeople need to excel in to achieve your sales goals?
   a. _____
   b. _____
   c. _____

4. List three things you could do immediately to build **higher levels of trust** and mega-credibility with your prospects and customers.
   a. _____
   b. _____
   c. _____

5. What three actions could your salespeople take to make **more persuasive and effective sales presentations**?
   a. _____
   b. _____
   c. _____

6. What three actions could you take, or incentives could you offer, to **get your prospects to buy sooner** rather than delaying a purchase decision?
a. _____
b. _____
c. _____

7. List three questions that you could ask to elicit a buying decision from an interested prospect.
a. _____
b. _____
c. _____

What one action are you going to take immediately to increase your sales?

_____
_____
_____
_____
_____
_____
_____
_____

About Brian

Brian Tracy has consulted for more than 1,000 companies and addressed more than 5,000,000 people in 5,000 talks and seminars throughout the US, Canada and 70 other countries worldwide. As a Keynote speaker and seminar leader, he addresses more than 250,000 people each year.

He has studied, researched, written and spoken for over 30 years in the fields of economics, history, business, philosophy and psychology. He is the top-selling author of over 90 books that have been translated into dozens of languages.

Brian speaks to corporate and public audiences on the subjects of Personal and Professional Development, including the executives and staff of many of America's largest corporations. His exciting talks and seminars on Leadership, Selling, Self-Esteem, Goals, Strategy, Creativity and Success Psychology bring about immediate changes and long-term results.

CHAPTER 2

BUILDING AN ACCOUNTING ENTERPRISE

BY JAMES THOMASSON

Success is a multifaceted concept that is measured in various ways. As we navigate through life, our perception of success evolves, influenced by our experiences, circumstances, and personal aspirations. In my own journey, I have come to understand that success is not solely determined by financial wealth or material possessions. Instead, it lies in finding contentment and fulfillment in what we do, free from unnecessary struggles. This realization has shaped my perspective on success, allowing me to thrive in any situation, regardless of the economy or external factors.

Growing up as the sixth of seven children in a family where financial resources were scarce, our definition of success was simple. The smallest joys, such as having a bowl of ice cream, made our days feel successful. My mother, married to a truck driver, faced the challenge of raising a large family on a truck driver's income and what she earned as an employee of a discount retail operation. While there is nothing wrong with being a truck driver, achieving financial stability without owning a trucking company or having a reliable team of drivers can be difficult. Working for someone else can still lead to success, but it requires exceptional skills and the ability to contribute to the success of one's superiors. However, success can manifest in different forms and can be achieved irrespective of the economy, time, or location.

Success begins with setting specific and tangible goals. These goals act as guideposts, allowing us to navigate our journey towards success. It is important for these goals to be adaptable, evolving alongside our personal growth and changing life circumstances. Merely stating vague aspirations, such as wanting to accumulate a million dollars, is insufficient. Setting a time limit for achieving our goals and breaking them down into smaller milestones facilitates a more concrete path to success.

However, it is crucial to ensure that our goals remain realistic. For instance, aiming to earn a million dollars within a year or relying solely on winning the lottery may not be achievable or sustainable. A better goal would be to plan to grow a business to a million-dollar business by the end of the year, backed by a specific innovative way to increase business.

Reflecting on my own upbringing in the 1960s and 1970s in South Alabama, I recall the challenges of living in a poor household. Both of my parents worked tirelessly, leaving the older children responsible for caring for the younger ones. Our two-bedroom house had a leaky roof, a shower falling through a rotten floor, and a dysfunctional vanity sink. Moreover, we lacked air conditioning during the sweltering summers, where temperatures would reach the upper 90s with near 100% humidity. Enduring such conditions was extremely uncomfortable, not to mention what challenges there were during the damp and cold winters. Yet, in our naivety, we did not realize the extent of our hardships.

As the years passed, my siblings and I transitioned into adolescence and adulthood. With little to lose, we all began setting our individual goals, embarking on our respective journeys towards success. However, setting goals alone is not enough. To transform dreams into reality, we must develop detailed plans. As Zig Ziglar once said, "Success is a destination, not a journey." The goal is the destination, and the plan is the journey. Our plans act as the vehicle that propels us towards our desired destinations. Without a well-structured plan, our goals remain mere fantasies, trapping us within a perpetual state of dreaming.

Observing the accomplishments of my older brother, who worked at McDonald's starting at the age of 19, inspired me to strive for entrepreneurial success. While his initial aspirations did not revolve around working at McDonald's, he gradually advanced within the company, eventually setting a goal to own a McDonald's franchise. Family members knew he was destined for success, perhaps before he knew it himself, but he formulated a comprehensive plan, constantly refining and adapting it along the way and in his own time.

Setting goals, creating plans, and taking action constitute an ongoing process. Success requires consistent implementation of our plans and the ability to adapt to the ever-changing environment, market trends, economic fluctuations, and personal circumstances.

During my high school days, I had the chance to clean and maintain the floor at the nearby city park before classes. Although the pay wasn't substantial, the park director needed assistance as her maintenance staff had quit. This experience taught me a valuable lesson. At the end of the year, I received a 1099-misc form from the city, indicating the amount I had earned as a contract laborer the previous year. I had always filed my own tax returns as a W2 employee, so I was unsure how to report this 'self-employed' income on my tax return, especially since I didn't consider myself self-employed. To address this, I took all my paperwork, including the 1099 form, to a tax franchise business. One of the employees manually entered my information on the federal tax form, and during the process, she asked about my state refund from Alabama the previous year. I informed her of the amount, and she entered it on the form. However, I objected, explaining that it wasn't taxable because I hadn't claimed it as an itemized deduction in the prior year.

Thankfully, she quickly acknowledged her mistake, exclaiming, "Oh, that's right!" and promptly erased it from the return. She correctly recorded the income from my contract work on the appropriate schedule, and it finally became clear to me where I should report such income. Realizing that the employee was unsure about properly preparing my state return, I decided to take matters into my own hands and dismissed her, completing the return myself. From this experience, I learned two important lessons: firstly, that contract labor qualifies as self-employment and should be reported accordingly, and secondly, that I was capable of preparing income tax returns as well as, if not better than, an experienced employee at the country's largest tax franchise.

In 1987, after completing my studies at the University of South Alabama, I secured a seasonal position at a local CPA firm. Unexpectedly, I was offered a job at a bank the following day. Although I had not intended to work two jobs simultaneously, I recognized the value of hard work in achieving my aspirations, even if I was uncertain about my ultimate destination. I worked at the CPA firm for eight tax seasons while simultaneously managing a full-time position as a credit manager at a local finance company.

Witnessing the success achieved by my siblings, who became accomplished entrepreneurs, I, too, aspired to embark on a similar path. Consequently, I left my banking job and sought the guidance of a business broker, who suggested investing in a laundromat. Intrigued by the idea of a business that seemingly operated independently, I purchased a laundromat, unaware of the challenges that lay ahead. As it turned out, the reality was far from the broker's portrayal. Working tirelessly and adapting my goals, I eventually sold the laundromat in 1998, realizing a profit.

In 1995, I acquired Accelerated Accounting, a local tax practice, recognizing the seasonal nature of the business as both an advantage and a disadvantage. While tax practices experience peak periods during tax seasons, generating substantial revenue, they can also suffer from significant lulls during the rest of the year. To overcome this challenge and ensure financial stability beyond April 15th, I established TBS Communications, a paging business, operating from the back of the laundromat. Although the decision may have seemed unconventional, I was willing to embrace hard work and seize opportunities that presented themselves.

With perseverance and dedication to my plan, both Accelerated Accounting and TBS Communications flourished. Recognizing the potential for growth in the paging industry, I acquired several other paging resellers, ultimately establishing one of the largest paging reseller networks along the upper Gulf Coast. Witnessing the success achieved through acquisitions, I applied a similar strategy to expand my accounting and tax practice. By 2001, TBS Communications had diversified into cell phones and pagers, prompting me to divest from the paging business and focus solely on accounting and cellular services. In 2003, I brought in a partner for the communications business and subsequently sold it to him in 2005, generating a substantial profit.

As the laundromat and TBS Communications became chapters of the past, I shifted my focus towards expanding Accelerated Accounting. Over the years, we transformed it into a comprehensive accounting enterprise, boasting five locations across Alabama, Florida, and Georgia. In our company, we hold to the policy of family first. Our fifteen employees have bought into that vision and are willing to do what is necessary for us to be successful.

When I bought Accelerated Accounting in 1995, the previous owner had one employee who had been there for five years prior to my purchase. She is still with us today. The firm I bought in 2007 also had one employee besides the owner, who had been there for the previous eight years. She told me, when I bought it, that she would work through the tax season and would not leave me 'high and dry.' She helped me transition the existing clients that first year and every year until she passed in 2022. She will always be an important part of our business family.

There is no way I could buy multiple practices and be the only one to take care of the client. Having the education and experience is not the entire formula for success in the service industry. Employing good people with those skills and providing outstanding customer service is the key to scaling your business and being more successful than you could ever be on your own. I have an awesome team, and my operations manager keeps me focused on building the business and being organized with the administrative duties.

Over the years, we have become experts in our field. Being students of our 'game,' we are the best in our niche in our market. The brother who is just older than I am started a carpet cleaning business in Houston, Texas, over forty years ago. His company is the best and most expensive carpet cleaner in the metropolitan area. He wasn't satisfied there. He wanted to help other carpet cleaners build their businesses. As he refined his goals and worked hard to become a highly successful business coach, he, too, strives to be the best at what he does.

'Givers Gain' is another principle we believe in. I first heard of this idea in BNI (Business Network International), a networking group I am involved in. It basically states that when you become a giver, the reward to you is more than the amount given. In our BNI, when we give business referrals to other members, the other members send you referrals in return. It doesn't seem logical, but it works.

Success does not happen by accident. We never wait for opportunity; we create it. When I find a practice for sale, I am ready. I can tell the seller how much I am willing to pay within fifteen minutes of our initial conversation (depending on due diligence and confirmation of what I was told). This way, I cut out the competition. The amount rarely deviates significantly from the original price originally quoted, but I am always ready for that price change as well. In many cases, the seller will actually finance the deal for you. This way, you can pay for the business with the profit of the business.

Despite encountering challenges such as the real estate market decline in 2008 and the global pandemic in 2020, we have continued to experience consistent growth, averaging over 20% annually the past four years mainly due to the employees that work with me. To them, I give all the glory.

Furthermore, I have strategically invested in commercial properties, owning two of the buildings housing our offices and an additional eight commercial buildings. To further accelerate our growth, we have partnered with a private equity company and are currently in the process of franchising our business, with the goal of selling fifty franchises within the next five years.

My mom worked hard until age 86 when the company she worked for closed its doors this year. I learned from her that hard work will get you started, but working smarter really pays off.

Regardless of how we individually define success, the key lies in setting goals, formulating detailed plans, diligently working towards those goals, and accumulating capital along the way. Success should not be dependent on the prevailing economic conditions or external circumstances. Rather, it is a result of our unwavering commitment to our goals, the resilience to adapt to changes, and the determination to overcome challenges. By embracing this approach, we can shape our own destinies and achieve success in any environment.

In conclusion, success is a multifaceted concept that encompasses more than just financial wealth or material possessions. It is a subjective notion that evolves over time, influenced by personal experiences, circumstances, and aspirations. True success lies in finding contentment and fulfillment in what we do, free from unnecessary struggles. It begins with setting specific and tangible goals, formulating detailed plans, and taking consistent action. Success is not determined solely by external factors but rather by our commitment, resilience, and ability to adapt to change. By embracing these principles, we can navigate our own paths to success, regardless of the economy or external circumstances.

About James

James Thomasson is an accomplished and forward-thinking accountant, consultant, entrepreneur, as well as the President and CEO of Accelerated Financial Services, INC. With an extraordinary career spanning several decades, he has consistently demonstrated his ability to think outside the box, delivering innovative solutions and driving business growth.

Before developing Accelerated Financial Services, Inc. to what it is today, James served as the President and CEO of TBS Communications, Inc., where he led the company to new heights of success through his visionary leadership and strategic acumen. His exceptional skills in financial management and business development have earned him a reputation as a trailblazer in business.

In addition to his corporate responsibilities, James also serves as the Chairman of the United Bank Advisory Board, where he provides invaluable insights and guidance on financial matters. He previously held the position of Chairman of the Saraland Area Chamber of Commerce, where he played a pivotal role in fostering economic growth and strengthening the local business community.

James' journey towards excellence began by working his way through college and earning a Bachelor of Science degree in Finance from the University of South Alabama. He started his own accounting practice in 1987 and since then, his entrepreneurial spirit has driven him to acquire ten different tax and accounting practices, establishing himself as a recognized authority on business acquisitions.

Throughout his illustrious career, James has consistently proven himself to be a visionary leader with a deep understanding of finance, business strategy, and the art of successful entrepreneurship. His passion for innovation, coupled with his extensive knowledge, has positioned him as a sought-after expert in the industry. James Thomasson's dedication, expertise, and unwavering commitment to excellence have earned him the respect and admiration of his peers and colleagues alike.

Learn more about James at:
- acceleratedaccounting.tax

CHAPTER 3

THE POWER OF ATTITUDE, MOTIVATION, AND COMMITMENT IN BUSINESS SUCCESS

BY PATRICK ZIEMER

It's tough to make predictions, especially about the future.
~ Yogi Berra

Since I graduated from college in 1973, I have, for the most part, been self-employed. I have operated businesses in several different industries. The list includes my family's funeral business, an ambulance service, screen and offset printing, marketing and advertising services, aviation sales and services, and most recently, medical device manufacturing and sales to the veterinary and human markets.

Over these years, there have been many times when the economy has been a challenging factor in the operation and profitability of my businesses. I have learned the breadth of the word economy. There are several ways that the economy can affect us. *Success in Any Economy* does not only deal with the world or the U.S. business economy, but it also deals with the local economy, your economic situation, or even the economic conditions in a particular industry. For this book, I will focus on my business activity since the 9/11 terrorist attacks and how I became and stayed successful in any economy.

In 1998, I took a job in the aviation jet charter business as a sales executive. The company operated Lear Jets that flew morning package overflow for UPS and then would sit idle. By mid-morning, somebody would refit the aircraft for passengers, and it was my job to secure charters for the aircraft. I was able to charter their jets all over the country. We grew from two to eleven aircraft, and the company soared. In 2001, I entered into a contract with Louisville International Airport to operate a charter and maintenance facility. In addition to air charter services, our primary service business was servicing overflow aircraft flying for UPS... then 9/11 hit and UPS cut their overflow aircraft needs from 120 per day to four, from 25 busy employees to no work. By February 2002, we closed to avoid total loss and bankruptcy, and I was on my own and needed to start over.

In June 2002, I began my PEMF journey by providing low-power PEMF equipment to the equine industry. PEMF uses Pulsed Electro-magnetic Frequencies to promote our body's overall health and wellness and enhance the body's ability to heal itself. It is interesting how new chapters build on old ones. In college, I'd worked around horses at a local racetrack. A friend in Canada, who knew that I had some horse experience, built low-powered PEMF therapy devices for horses and asked me to help him sell them. "Don't go straight to Churchill Downs," he warned me. "Wait to learn the racing community." My economic situation could have been better, and I had no time to wait and slowly learn about the equine therapy business. So I went straight to Churchill Downs, where a trainer agreed to break me in. "Come every day and shadow me," he said. "I'll tell you who to talk to, how things work, where to be, and when to be there."

In a month, I had camaraderie among the horse people and a nice start to business in the horse world—albeit less profitable than aviation. Total immersion and learning at top speed allowed me to improve my economy and begin to build what would become today's Magna Wave and Aura Wellness businesses.

I traveled extensively throughout the United States and Canada – selling and training others to use PEMF equipment. During the Spring and Summer months, I would work out of my home in Louisville, which worked well while building my book of business. I would work in Florida during the winter season, covering Ocala, Tampa, Wellington, and Miami. So it was hotels or apartments as a base of operation. The problem was that, in Florida, most apartments required a six-month lease. Initially, this seemed like it was fine, but I soon found myself with apartments in Ocala, Tampa, and Wellington. The apartments created a huge economic strain that was hindering growth.

My solution and pivot were to rent an RV, allowing me to work the state more easily and economically. In 2004 my wife decided to retire from teaching and travel with me. We sold our home, purchased a larger RV bus, and began a full-time five-year journey around the United States building our business. During this time, business was growing, but we could have done better in the Aviation industry. With the feeling that the business would continue to grow, we stayed the course and continued traveling.

As we continued our travels and observed other businesses, we learned that we needed more credibility and authority in the veterinary industry. Our devices worked, but the education process was daunting. In the 1800s, the AMA moved several modalities out of mainline medicine in the United States. Our modality of Electro-Medicine was no longer considered mainline medicine in the United States. While PEMF is a mainline of medicine worldwide, it was not considered viable in the United States.

In 2003, I began to embrace the Internet as a form of communication with new and existing customers by utilizing

Yahoo and AOL chat groups. To improve my credibility, I would host conversations with doctors, therapists, and practitioners of complimentary modalities. This process improved my credibility as a professional and not just a salesman. When Facebook launched in 2004 and began to mature as a platform, I embraced its profile, page, and group elements as a digital communications platform with my customers. I also jumped on the YouTube bandwagon in 2005 and began posting video testimonials, interviews, and answers to questions. The use of digital media greatly improved my credibility and authority in the PEMF industry.

In 2010, I could stop full-time travel and work from our home base in Kentucky. Due to our digital presence, Magna Wave has grown to become a domestic and international leader in the PEMF industry. While in-person contact is still vital, our foundation and growth are tied directly to digital communications and relationships. Today these tools are useful and viable to anyone wanting to grow their business in any economy.

A big change came for us in 2007 when we switched from Low-Power PEMF to High-Voltage, High-power PEMF Devices. The difference between low-power and high-power PEMF devices is the speed of results. The results of a high-power device occur in minutes instead of the days it takes with a low-powered machine. With this new device, which I branded as Magna Wave, I began to provide therapy treatments and sell devices.

Providing the treatments soon became an obstacle, because I was known around the country with credibility and authority, as an equipment salesperson, not a therapist. Even though I have a secondary college degree in microbiology, anatomy, and pathology, some people felt that I did not have the qualifications to be a therapist. As a result, my top customer challenge became the discussions on my education as a basis for my understanding and qualification to provide the therapy. While sharing my background helped, the real catalyst for the business growth was that the treatment worked. Plain and simple, *it works!*

From my beginning with high-powered devices, I was a distributor for a third-party manufacturer. The manufacturer was one of two that I could have chosen. I based my choice on continually being told that FDA and international clearances were coming. While the supplier repeatedly promised that these approvals were forthcoming, they never came to fruition during my association. I had to create the authenticity needed on my own while waiting on the process to be completed by the manufacturer. It became my mission to establish the company as the leader and authority in the PEMF space.

First, I created the brand (Magna Wave) which became one of the most recognized PEMF brands in the veterinary therapy space. Second, I started the first training and certification course in the industry. Implementing the certification course helped increase sales by 40% within thirty days. This growth solidified my desire to test and validate the equipment fully. I became further involved in social media, video production, and live stream events, and participated in seven books to continually improve credibility and acceptance.

The business grew from six figures to eight figures within four years. The staff grew from myself and my wife to six employees, including my daughter and son. Along the way, we began to work with more people, including animal owners and professional athletes, who are known to use products off-label that work for their recovery and resilience. The problem was that, with humans, we could not make any specific claims or freely sell into the human market. Only six PEMF devices are FDA-cleared, and few manufacturers meet the required GMP (Good Manufacturing Practices) and clearances for human distribution.

At this point, we had reached a critical juncture and decided on our future: either remain as a veterinary-only machine or upgrade to the human arena. While remaining as a veterinary company would have been the most straightforward choice, we determined that we needed to authenticate our devices to the FDA standards our customers continually requested.

While this was a big challenge, a second one presented itself at this time that ultimately would completely change our processes and products. Because of competitors' movements, a mid-price range hole developed in our product line, significantly impacting sales efforts. The manufacturer told us they would fill the gap with a new competitive product within three months. After six months, we found another manufacturer with a product that would fill the hole and allow us to be entirely competitive again. While this allowed us to maintain our sales and growth, our current manufacturer was unhappy with our need to move in a different direction. Ultimately, it took four years for the manufacturer to bring a new device to market.

Over time, the machine from the new manufacturer became the lead device in our product offering. The new device supplier needed to expand operations to meet our needs, and they did not have the desire to do so. As a result, I took the third key step for our success and took control of the manufacturing. I purchased the company and moved the manufacturing to our home office in Louisville, Kentucky. We decided to re-engineer all product offerings to be manufactured and safety tested to meet FDA U.S. requirements and export standards. This process would take a year to complete, but it has taken more than three and a half years.

While the business continued to grow, we did not expect the U.S. or global economy to get in the way. Still, we did experience a couple of serious challenges due to the economy. The crash in 2008 / 2009 basically wiped out about 30% of our business. To some, our products were for the luxury veterinary market, and many customers were not there or certainly cautious with their spending. We made two pivots that brought the customers back and allowed us to continue to grow in the rough economy.

Typically an equine session with our equipment would cost around $125.00 and last for 30 minutes to an hour while we treated the full body of the horse. Customers were balking at the cost, so the pivot was to treat the horse in sections. We would treat the area in need for $40.00. It worked well as customers jumped at the opportunity to save money and still get the primary areas treated. What happened is that we would treat three or four horses in an hour and would still make the standard $125.00 that we needed for our time. This move allowed us and our practitioners to continue to grow their businesses.

The second pivot was that we began to offer short-term rentals and an in-house rent-to-own program. Our primary device price at the time was $20,000.00, so with the rental pivot, our market would have dramatically increased. My promise to my manufacturers at the time was that if I rented a machine, it would not be returned to the factory but would stay with us until paid in full. Because of continued economic issues, customers returned 15% of the devices. Still, we could sell them at a significant discount or re-rent them to other customers. These maneuvers allowed Magna Wave to prosper during the downturn in the economy.

Next came COVID in 2020, and we thought that with the lockdowns, we would not survive the pandemic. At this point, we had around 4000 practitioners who were in the same boat as us. Our pivot saved the company and allowed the company and practitioners to thrive. We pulled a page from the rental playbook to help our practitioners. The horse and pet owners were locked down but still needed to care for their animals.

Practitioners could not readily treat but could still communicate with their customers. We started a rent-to-rent program with our practitioners, allowing them to rent a device from us and re-rent it to their customers. The practitioners loved the program because they could continue to operate, and the customers loved it because they could continue to help their animals with this program. Because of this pivot, we could continue our growth during the pandemic.

As a result of these pivots during hard economic times, Magna Wave has continued to grow at a rate of 12 to 15% year over year. We made the Inc 5000 list of fastest-growing privately-owned companies in 2021 and 2022 and have no plans to slow down.

Clients ask what I and the company do to stay on top of the momentum. My answer is that I follow my personal CAMP rules.

- C – You must stay committed to your business and goals.
- A – You must keep a good and positive attitude and project that attitude to your clients.
- M – Always work to remain motivated by reading books and working with mentors.
- P – Always be prepared to pivot to keep on track.

When I follow my CAMP rules it becomes much easier to look into the future. Join me today at CAMP!

About Pat

Patrick Ziemer is the owner of Magna Wave PEMF and Aura Wellness. Pat has been working full time with PEMF since 2002. The company's therapy devices are used extensively on racehorses, performance horses, and professional athletes. Several recent Kentucky Derby winners and numerous world champions in many horse disciplines utilize the therapy regularly. Many NFL, MLB, NBA, NHL, and MLS teams utilize Magna Wave Therapy.

In 2007, Pat began working with high powered PEMF devices. He branded the devices as Magna Wave and hit the road marketing the Magna Wave brand. Since 2007, the company has placed over 4000 Magna Wave devices into the market for private and professional use. In 2019, he began the process of having his devices cleared by the FDA and CE marked for international distribution. One device is now registered with the FDA and three more are on course for FDA 510(k) clearance by the third quarter of 2023. Magna Wave and Aura Wellness now services the human, small animal, and equine markets.

Follow Pat on:

- LinkedIn @PatrickZiemer

CHAPTER 4

ESCAPE ARTIST

BY PAUL HERBKA

Success in business takes many paths. Some paths are focused on sales growth and some are focused on putting together the right team, while other paths emphasize creating better relationships with customers and vendors. Though all of those are important, one of the most vital paths is taking stock of yourself.

We allow many personal factors in our lives to hold us back from being the powerhouses we can be, which in turn can affect our business aspirations. You may be the key player in your business, but you probably still have areas in your life that you could recognize and work on that will help propel you to that next level of success.

There are three areas that can hold people back from success in their jobs, businesses, or lives: fear of failure, negative self-talk, and being inauthentic.

We often place these limitations on ourselves no matter what level we occupy in our career. You could be the one who does the grunt work at the company or you could be the top person or you might wear both hats. You might already be a successf entrepreneur or are preparing to launch a side gig or busin You might be managing a team or looking to build or matter who you are, it's important to do the work to move past these limitations and become who you are meant to be.

LET'S DIVE IN!

1. Fear of Failure

Fear of failure prevents you from taking action and taking risks. In your personal life, you might avoid trying something new because you may be embarrassed. What if someone sees that you aren't perfect? Guess what? You're not perfect! None of us are perfect!

Fear of failure in business can hold you and your great ideas back. You might end up looking just like all of the other employees when in fact you are designed to be the standout employee.

If you have a fear of failure, take a look back on your life. Did someone once tell you that you were worthless and you believed it? Did you have a bad experience at work after you made a suggestion? Do you worry that the direction of your business will fail if you try something bigger or different than what you're doing now?

Those are legitimate concerns. But ask yourself, do you like where you are in life when this fear holds you back? Do you have bigger aspirations? Do you want to be seen as the leader you know you are? Holding yourself back honors no one. If we let our fears cloud our dreams, we will always be looking for the sun.

If a fear of failure is holding you back, then you may be depriving yourself of some wonderful adventures and opportunities. You are made for greatness! Don't let your fears stop you. Allow yourself the freedom to be who you are and to spotlight what bring to the business and to the world.

Fa not the enemy; it's just part of the process.

Angela was a one of several managers for a large company. While she brought many positive things to her company, she let her fear of failure hold her back. She stayed quiet in meetings afraid she'd make a mistake or suggest a wrong idea or even look incompetent. Her fear of failure, fear of taking risks, and fear of embarrassment left her following the pack instead of leading it.

Finally, one day during a meeting she knew she had a great idea that would change the course of the group and positively impact the company. Even with her knees shaking, she drew on her courage and spoke up. She was timid and quiet at first, but then she noticed that the others were actually listening to her. They were nodding their encouragement and agreement. Her plan was accepted and she was put in charge of it. It allowed her colleagues and boss to see her a in a new light. She blossomed into a leader as she ran with her idea. Relationships with customers and vendors improved. Sales increased. Higher bonuses were handed out.

Angela was given the credit for her idea and the implementation of it, and the executives took notice of her leadership.

2. Negative Self-Talk
We all talk to ourselves. Sometimes we say things like "you've got this!" or "great job!" Other times we say negative things about ourselves. That can sound like "you don't know what you're doing" or "you don't deserve success" or "who do you think you are?" When you tune in to the audio files playing in your mind, do you find yourself listening and paying attention to the uplifting thoughts, or the negative ones?

Negative self-talk can be very damaging. It can rob you of confidence and cause anxiety. It can be a barrier in your professional and personal life.

The trouble with negative self-talk is that we start to believe it. We begin to believe that we're stupid, we don't deserve things, and all of the other negative things we tell ourselves. What's the antidote? Reprogramming your inner self-talk with positive affirmations. This is where you tell yourself: I am strong. I am smart. I am allowed to learn. I am powerful. I am a person of character and integrity. I am healthy. I am free of my fears and limiting beliefs. I am firmly focused on my goals. I am allowed to make mistakes. I am worthy. I deserve success in all I do. I bring value to my business. I am brave, bold, and authentic. I am enough.

Some people think this process is silly, but it works. Give it a try and watch what happens in your life.

For years, Patrick indulged in negative self-talk. He didn't think he was worthy of success. He listened to the inner voice that told him he was stupid, couldn't do it, would be embarrassed, that no one would accept him.

He began to internalize that negative self-talk. He really wanted to launch his own business but didn't believe he could. He knew he had a great idea that would be profitable and his true desire was to become an entrepreneur. He talked the big talk about his dreams for his business and all the while he worked in a job he hated.

Patrick heard a speaker on the topic of positive affirmations. At first, he thought it was just a bunch of hooey. There was no way that saying nice things to yourself could possibly make a difference in your attitude, which in turn would affect your actions.

His family began telling him to start his business or quit talking about it. Thinking back to that speaker and the stories he heard that day, he decided he had nothing to lose by creating positive affirmation statements.

After he wrote them, Patrick hung his positive affirmations on the bathroom mirror, had a copy on his phone, and at his desk. He began to say them aloud every day. It didn't take long before his mindset began to shift. He began to believe the affirmations, and those beliefs helped to give him the confidence to take the leap and launch his business. Now, years later, Patrick is a successful entrepreneur. When asked about his success, he credits the role positive affirmations had in helping to change his mindset and his confidence level so he could go after his dreams.

Please, take some time to write out your affirmations. Post them on the bathroom mirror. Put time on your daily calendar and say them aloud. And then start believing those things about yourself! You'll be unstoppable!

3. Hiding Your Authentic Self
People want to see the real you. They want to know your story, your good ideas, your path to success, and the impact you make on others.

Too often, we are being who we think others want us to be. Let that sink in. We are being who we think others want us to be. If we do that, then we are playing a role, much like an actor.

In life, it's important to be the real you. It fosters trust and creates personal, rather than transactional, relationships. Your business relationships will be more fruitful. Your personal relationships will be based on authenticity.

How do you feel when you know someone isn't being their authentic self with you? Do you think they are being phony? Is it like they are putting up a façade?

Wouldn't you rather be with someone who is being authentic? Others feel the same way about you. They want to see your authentic self.

Rebecca thought she was a great manager who ruled her

department rigorously. She didn't take excuses from employees. They were there to work hard and put their employment above anything else. It's what Rebecca did and expected the others who worked for her to do the same.

No one dared to take a vacation day. They came to work sick. They worked extra hours without pay (because she forced them to) and they took on additional projects (because they felt they had no choice).

Rebecca thought this was how to run a department based on her experience and the training she received from other managers.

What Rebecca didn't know was that most of her team was looking for positions with other companies. They were fed up with her as a manager and her "policies."

Even though Rebecca was proud of her department's accomplishments, she felt that she was deceiving herself. In her life outside of work, Rebecca was a compassionate, generous woman. It was such a dichotomy. Rebecca felt that she couldn't be her true self, her authentic self, because she'd be thought of as soft. She assumed her department's work would suffer. The stress of being these two people began to take a toll on Rebecca.

She finally decided that she could no longer be who others expected her to be while at work. Rebecca chose to be her authentic self. At first, people were surprised at the change.

Rebecca decided that her staff was going to work regular hours and that when other managers wanted her department to take on more work, she would say no and create boundaries to protect her employees.

She became empathetic. She encouraged people to take vacations. When someone was sick, she showed compassion by encouraging them to take off from work and had a hot meal sent to them. If someone had another obligation, that person was encouraged to fulfill it.

It took some time for things to turn around. Slowly her staff began to see and recognize Rebecca's authentic self. They began to enjoy working for and with her and stopped looking for other jobs. When Rebecca allowed her true self to be revealed, she was rewarded with genuine dedication and hard work. The group's pride in their work shone through.

Rebecca became one of the most powerful and sought after managers in her industry after she dedicated herself to being authentic.

Too many times we are encouraged or expected to be who others want us to be, even if it goes against who we think we should be. We split ourselves into two when we do that. It weighs on us and creates stress in our lives.

You are too valuable to hide the real you. Start owning your authentic self and share it with the world. Be who you are and who you're meant to be! Be your authentic self and see who you can inspire and impact. How will you share the real you with others?

NEXT STEPS

We all have limitations. Many times, they are the three mentioned here: *fear of failure*, *negative self-talk*, and *hiding our authentic selves*. Letting these restrictions hold us back in our lives is not beneficial for us nor the people around us.

Imagine the additional success you'll have after you unlock these restrictions. The joy and satisfaction will be much like finding the last digit to a lock you've been trying to open for months or years.

When you learn to embrace and conquer your limitations, it's like you become an escape artist. You will escape what's holding you back so you can go on to bigger and better things and have greater success.

You are meant to be bold. Courageous. A risk-taker. A master at relationships. Someone who believes in themselves.

Are you ready to level up and overcome these limitations?

It's time to take action.

Filling out the following three objectives can help you work free from your limitations:

(i). What small step will you take today that moves you out of your comfort zone?
_____
_____

(ii). Write one positive affirmation to say aloud daily.
I am _____
_____

(iii). How will you show your authentic self today?
_____
_____

It's time to create your next-level success!

About Paul

Paul Herbka masterfully guides entrepreneurs and business executives who want to accelerate their businesses in meaningful and impactful ways and who want to transform their strengths into massive success. As a business coach, award-winning speaker, and author, Paul has assisted clients exceed goals, receive accolades, and break records.

Paul Herbka, The Coach: Paul is equally comfortable working with individuals and teams. Whether you are an entrepreneur or part of an established organization, if you want to become a better version of yourself to help your business thrive, Paul is the coach for you. He will help you identify and overcome your blind spots, focus on income producing activities, and encourage you to see yourself as the superstar you are.

If you are managing a team in a small or large company, you can count on Paul to help you bring that team together so they are all running toward the same goal. He identifies the strengths and weaknesses of each individual and develops, with you, a plan to accelerate your business growth. You'll learn secrets to leveraging the team's skills to maximize effectiveness. Visit his website for a complimentary coaching session.

Paul Herbka, The Speaker and Trainer: Paul's winning presentation style is the best mix of learning and laughter. When Paul shares his sense of humor with an audience, you can be assured that the group is gaining valuable knowledge and strategies with a side of fun! He is equally comfortable and highly experienced in presenting to groups of any size, small or large, local or international. Bring Paul in for your next training or speaking engagement to boost knowledge on these and other topics: Communication and Teamwork, Breaking Through Limitations, and Building Endless Referrals for Your Business.

Paul Herbka, The Man: He began his career in IT with IBM and later specialized in cybersecurity. After 30 years in the industry, he knows his stuff. He has successfully launched multiple businesses, led global development and training teams, and coached individuals and companies. Paul lives in Colorado with his wife and enjoys the bounty of nature that surrounds them and roots for the home teams. He is a worldwide traveler with many stories to share. He always appreciates a good joke – especially the occasional harmless practical ones!

Contact Paul Herbka today – whether to be a dynamic speaker or an empowering coach – and let him boost you and your organization to the next level:

- **paulherbka.com**

CHAPTER 5

THE PITFALLS OF HIRING FRIENDS

BY DR. HEIDI GREGORY-MINA

"You don't need friends who become coworkers; you need coworkers who become family." I made the mistake of initially thinking that hiring friends was a great idea when I began hiring employees. We already knew each other and got along; however, over time, they began taking advantage of our friendship. They started coming in late, canceling, or rescheduling clients, and initially, they would ask for permission, but eventually, it became a notification. I found it difficult to talk to them about their performance and how it was impacting the business. I was always worried that this would destroy our friendship, and my personality didn't lend itself well to difficult conversations.

So, I let things slide, but it was hurting the business and led to resentment towards our friendship. I also recognized that there was fault on both sides. While their actions were not appropriate, it was also my responsibility to address the situation.

FOCUS ON SHARED VALUES, WORK ETHIC, AND CLEAR EXPECTATIONS

A better approach to building a successful team is to focus on hiring co-workers who share your values, work ethic, and possess the necessary skills for the job. While it is great to have a friendly and positive work environment, it is essential to maintain professional boundaries and establish clear expectations for performance and behavior. It is also crucial to foster a culture of open and honest communication where constructive feedback can be given and received without damaging relationships. This will help ensure that everyone is accountable and responsible for their work and the success of the business. As a leader, I strive to work with employees who value positive and constructive feedback and cultivate a culture of appreciation as this is how we can grow and learn.

Unfortunately, I learned this approach 'the hard way', such as the time I hired someone to run our canine rehabilitation business based on a referral from a friend, without vetting the candidate thoroughly. She disclosed that she was still in school but would have her full certification shortly. I was caught up in the moment and excited to have someone, so I said it would be fine and did not really think it through. Since we were in our pre-launch phase, there were tasks that needed to be completed that were not job-specific. We became quick friends, went to lunch often, attended fun events with our dogs, and I even had her over to the house a few times.

After working for about six months, I discovered that she had more schooling left than what she had disclosed. As the canine rehabilitation business was just starting and business was slow, she started taking advantage of her situation by booking one client in the morning and another in the afternoon, then stating in between clients that she was "cleaning" and doing "paperwork." I spoke with her about booking clients closer together because I could not afford to pay her for all the time in between without clients. She agreed and booked clients closer together for a while but then fell back into her old habits. Soon after, I woke up to an email from her stating that she was leaving immediately.

I quickly realized I had trusted her and given her too much power too quickly. I also considered her a friend but realized that the feeling was not reciprocated and that she was just watching out for her own good. She had quietly informed clients that she was leaving and asked them to contact her directly for future appointments. I found myself at a loss with some customers not returning, which hurt the canine rehabilitation business, as it was challenging to find someone with the necessary skills and certification to work in canine rehabilitation.

It took a while to rebuild this clientele, and the prospect of doing it again was daunting. However, I used this as a learning opportunity for future hires. Now, I hire slowly, place more value on their "drive" and "attitude", and do not solely hire a candidate based on their experience or certification to do the job.

VET EMPLOYEES THOROUGHLY AND CONSIDER JOB LOADING

Building a strong team with the right people in the right positions is critical, but it requires a deeper understanding of what that entails. To start, we must assess our own strengths and weaknesses to inform future hiring decisions. We ultimately want to build a team of employees that complement one another's skill sets. However, after onboarding a new employee, we may discover that the individual doesn't fit the company culture or sub-culture. Immediate termination isn't the only solution, and it can be costly for the organization. Instead, we should consider horizontal and vertical job loading as options.

Horizontal job loading involves adding new responsibilities to an employee's current job. This strategy can be an effective way to help the employee develop new skills and gain experience that they may not have had before. It also shows that the organization values the employee and is willing to invest in their growth and development. Vertical job loading involves promoting the employee to a new position with increased responsibilities and higher pay. This option is appropriate when an employee has demonstrated exceptional performance and has the potential to take on more significant roles within the organization. This can also help to retain high-performing employees and reduce turnover.

An example of effectively utilizing horizontal loading occurred when an employee was struggling to process feedback and learn from it, due to a lack of emotional intelligence, even with assistance. We considered letting her go but recognized that this would be costly for the organization as we would lose her tacit knowledge. As we explored alternatives, the idea came to mind: "Wouldn't it be great if we had a position where all she had to do was talk?" It then dawned on us that we did have such a position: our patient intake line. We presented this idea to the manager for that area, who agreed, and the employee was enthusiastic about the opportunity. In her new role, she thrived, and it turned out to be a win-win for everyone. We retained an employee we had invested in, and she was able to use her strengths to help the organization become more effective.

However, not all scenarios lend themselves to horizontal or vertical job loading, and sometimes we need to allow our employees to move on to grow and pursue their dreams. When I worked in healthcare, there was an employee who was being considered for a promotion to Finance Manager, but I sensed that she was not as excited about it as I had expected. I asked her to lunch later that week and discovered that her true passion was to become a nurse. After a lot of discussion, I encouraged her to pursue her dreams, and she eventually became a Nurse Practitioner. While she was in school, she continued to work part-time and helped cross-train new employees. Upon graduation, she accepted a full-time position with the hospital, which was the best outcome for everyone involved.

DEALING WITH REJECTION AND PERSONAL BIASES

Being aware of our biases when building teams is crucial for creating a diverse and inclusive workplace. Unconscious biases are biases that we hold but are not aware of. They are formed from our experiences, background, culture, and other societal factors, and they can influence our decision-making processes, actions, and behaviors without our conscious knowledge.

An example of an unconscious bias is the affinity bias. Affinity bias is when we favor people who we perceive to be similar to us in terms of background, interests, or personality. For example, a manager may be more likely to hire someone who went to the same university as they did, even if the candidate is less qualified than other applicants. This bias can result in a lack of diversity in the workplace and can prevent qualified individuals from being hired or promoted.

To truly promote cultural diversity and inclusivity in the workplace, we need to be aware of our own biases and actively work to address them. This was a lesson I learned when building teams in the past. While I did not intentionally select only male leaders, I realized that my unconscious biases had led me to make those decisions. After this was brought to my attention, I made a conscious effort to select leaders based on a diverse set of qualities, which ultimately resulted in greater creativity and innovation within my teams. By actively working to address our biases, we can create a more diverse and inclusive workplace where all employees feel valued and supported.

Experiencing biases in the workplace can be disheartening, and it can be challenging to navigate rejection when we suspect biases played a role. This was a reality I faced in my own career, where I felt that my gender was prioritized over my skills and qualifications. A few years ago, I went through a rigorous interview process for a promotion at a major university. After making it through three rounds, I was confident that the job offer was within reach. However, after waiting for what seemed like an eternity, I received the news that someone else had been chosen for the position. I was in shock, and my self-confidence took a hit.

A couple of months later, I ran into someone from the interview panel who told me that they wished I had gotten the job. In our conversation, she revealed that the only reason the other candidate was chosen was because I was of childbearing age, and they were concerned about potential maternity leave. This was a painful reality to confront, as it's one thing to be aware of biases but another to hear them spoken aloud. However, I learned that it's essential to handle rejection with grace and professionalism, even when faced with the painful truth behind the decision-making process.

HIRING FOR PERSON-JOB FIT AND FOSTERING EMPLOYEE GROWTH

As I move forward, I no longer hire friends. The first thing I look for is person-job fit, and then I consider their skill set. By focusing on person-job fit, we are ensuring that we are hiring someone whose personality aligns with the organization's culture because personality cannot be taught or changed. We can learn to become more self-aware and manage our personality. While skill set is important, many skills can be taught, so this becomes a secondary focus. Providing employees the opportunity to learn and grow will help them stay committed to the organization.

When hiring, I focus on building a solid working relationship by getting to know candidates, asking a lot of questions, and taking it slow. Many times, I will begin with a freelance approach before making a commitment. This approach allows me to develop trust with the person over time, and as a result, we get to know each other naturally. These employees organically move from the out-group to the in-group throughout this process. I have found that employees hired through this method are more engaged with the organization and provide higher levels of discretionary effort. Additionally, taking the time to understand the individual's values and career goals can help me better align their strengths and interests with the organization's needs. This creates a more fulfilling and purpose-driven work experience for the employee, which in turn leads to better performance and retention.

Recently, I was searching for someone to help me manage my social media accounts. During the interviewing process, I connected with a candidate on a personal level. However, the idea of someone else managing my social media presence made me feel uneasy. I wondered if my initial impression was accurate and if I could trust this person. So, I decided to take things slowly and invest time in getting to know her better. At first, she helped me sort out my branding, then we began weekly meetings, and finally, I had her start creating content for me. As we worked together, we developed a professional and personal relationship. Now, I feel entirely comfortable with her and would trust her to take over my accounts without hesitation. This experience has reinforced my belief that establishing a relationship with potential employees is critical for building trust and engagement.

This investment of time was definitely worth it because it led to a valuable long-term relationship. Taking the time to create these types of organizational relationships can lead to a strong corporate culture built on shared beliefs and values. It's important to remember that building relationships takes time and effort, but it can have a significant impact on the success of the organization. As leaders today, we need to show a level of vulnerability to our employees to build authentic relationships based on trust and transparency. With many work environments remaining virtual or hybrid, our employees require a higher level of autonomy, and building strong relationships with them can foster a sense of trust and motivation that ultimately benefits the organization.

In conclusion, the pitfalls of hiring friends in the workplace can be detrimental to both personal relationships and business operations. While it is essential to maintain a friendly and positive work environment, it is equally important to establish professional boundaries and clear expectations for performance and behavior. By focusing on hiring co-workers who share values, work ethic, and possess the necessary skills for the job, we can build a strong and cohesive team that works together towards achieving shared goals. Thoroughly vetting employees and considering horizontal and vertical job loading can also contribute to creating a positive work culture and promoting employee growth and development.

While it can be difficult to navigate the complexities of managing both personal relationships and professional responsibilities, with clear communication, accountability, and a commitment to growth, we can create a workplace that is both productive and fulfilling. Remember, you don't need friends who become coworkers; you need coworkers who become family.

About Dr. Heidi

Dr. Heidi Gregory-Mina is a highly regarded business psychologist, esteemed professor, and accomplished author known for her exceptional ability to combine academic research with practical applications. Drawing on her extensive real-world experience, she offers her clients and readers valuable insights into the science of human behavior, empowering them to enhance their performance and achieve their objectives through workshops, seminars, consulting, and speaking engagements.

As the host of "Dr. Heidi The Business Psychologist" podcast, Dr. Heidi shares her expertise with a broad audience, exploring topics related to business psychology, leadership, and personal development. .

With over 20 years of experience working for nonprofits prior to entering higher education, Dr. Heidi is a multifaceted professional who brings a unique perspective to her work. Her diverse background and dedication to social responsibility are reflected in her belief in the power of education and community engagement as catalysts for positive change.

Dr. Heidi can be reached at:

- drheidigregorymina.com.

CHAPTER 6

LIVING AND WORKING WITH TRUE AUTHENTICITY IN THE WORKPLACE

BY JAMES RADFORD

From my childhood up to decades of service in support of my country and many more in the corporate world, I've aimed to live and work within the framework of authenticity. Everyone has their tentpole issue, their harbor in the storm, the hat upon which everything they do must hang.

For me, it's *authenticity*.

But what is authenticity? We could walk down the street right now and ask 100 random people (Jay Leno style) what authenticity means to them, and we would get 100 different answers. So, I'm not here to tell you what authenticity is; I'm here to tell you what authenticity has meant and does mean to me.

TRUST CONSULTING SERVICES

I called my company Trust Consulting Services purely for that word—trust. I wanted clients and partners to know they could trust in the services we provide, that they could trust me, and that they could trust my team. In everything we do, we aim to build, foster, and nurture trust.

But how does trust dovetail with authenticity?

Trust | verb, to believe that someone is good and honest and will not harm you, or that something is safe and reliable.

Authenticity | noun: worthy of acceptance or belief as conforming to or based on fact; conforming to an original so as to reproduce essential features.

From the standpoint of doing business, it stands to reason that being good, honest, safe, reliable, and conforming to the facts are the best attributes you could possess. This is what I wanted for my business. If I can live up to those principles, I can serve my clients and my employees well.

However, there's more to the story than a simple glossary of good ideas. How can I translate these concepts into a business that functions properly in all phases?

AN EVER-CHANGING MARKET

The marketplace changes all day, every day. There's never a moment when the market isn't shifting under our feet with an almost tectonic ferocity that challenges businesses, managers, and team members alike. But, what we do in response to the market speaks to our authenticity.

Take a look at the roller coaster Mercedes experienced in the early 2000s. At one time, Mercedes was considered the titan of all automobiles (even the luxury supercars), a byword for quality, the car everyone wanted to drive. Customer service was top notch. Every car was flawless. The firm reportedly spent around $1 million EVERY DAY on R&D to make sure that the car you got was the spitting image of perfection. The S-Class was the first production car to roll out a massive range of standard features like anti-lock brakes, passenger airbags, and more. The mind-bending statistics go on and on.

However, the C-Suite at Mercedes (one day) decided that, in the words of famed British television presenter, Jeremy Clarkson, its vehicles were 'needlessly over-engineered' and chose to pull back more profit for shareholders and executives. Not surprisingly, customer service fell through the floor, drivers weren't all that impressed, and sales suffered.

All the money that Mercedes saved because it chose not to do things the 'right way' was all wasted when it wasn't meeting its sales goals and irritating customers. The market shifted and Mercedes chose to rest on its laurels, believing that the sales pipeline would never dry up—but it could dry up without warning.

YOU CAN'T UNDERCUT THE MARKET

At Trust Consulting Services, we don't attempt to undercut the market, underbid our competitors, or change our values as the market shifts. What you see is what you get. When you're referred to us, you get the very same quality everyone else has experienced.

Our firm is no different than it was when I signed my first contract with the Department of Transportation in 2015. We established a solid relationship which stands to this day because the DOT knows that we are both authentic and true to our core values.

Therefore, authenticity is consistent from day one to the present. If you're truly unflappable, you can build relationships with companies and clients, even going beyond the boardroom into your personal life, at times growing along with clients for decades at a time.

Who doesn't want to see their kids grow up with the children of those they admire and respect, or make lifelong friends based on what started as a simple contract? These things don't happen by accident—they're the result of true, abiding authenticity.

Now that you know you cannot undercut the market, look at all the money you aren't losing due to bad contracts or underpromised services. Yes, some aspects of the market will get cheaper, you'll see competitors offering lower quality at a lower price, but that's not who you are.

Rather than chasing the money, you can be true to yourself and your business model, expecting to be paid properly for the goods or services you provide, understanding that that quality will be rewarded with repeat business and longstanding relationships.

THE TRUTH IS FREE

As authenticity points back to the truth, it's important for us to lean into the value of the truth.

- The truth is worth its weight in gold.

- The truth emboldens us.

- The truth makes for wise decisions.

- And...the truth is free.

When we work with clients and customers, we must give them the truth, even when it doesn't result in a profit. There will be times when you simply shouldn't bid on a contract or take a job because there's no reason to believe you could or should accept it. At times, the price isn't right. Oftentimes, you don't have the personnel. Many times, you simply aren't the right fit. You don't have the expertise, and that's alright.

Sending your clients away with the truth speaks to your

authenticity. You're being true to what you can and cannot do. I can assure you that those prospects will return or offer referrals because you were, at the very least, honest.

That level of honesty becomes a calling card for your business, just as it is at Trust Consulting Services. We aren't here to make the most money, offer the lowest price, provide the most services simultaneously, etc. We're here to give our customers, clients, and prospects the truth, even when they don't want to hear it.

For example, you may find that a client is asking for far less than they need. You're not telling them, "do this and that" because you want the cash. You're being honest because, "if we only install four cameras in your 200,000 square foot warehouse, we simply can't see everything. Or, "if we only post one guard at the desk of your 14-floor office building, we cannot manage every eventuality."

At the same time, your honesty might hurt your wallet because it's the right thing to do—it's authentic of you to do right by your clients. "You don't need a rotation of 15 security guards for your 1,200 square foot doctor's office." Yes, it would be nice to sign a massive contract with that client, but what are you doing if you post a dozen guards at a tiny office? You know it's wrong, and eventually, they'll realize they're overpaying for something they don't need.

Instead, offer the right level of service at the appropriate price. In time, that business will turn into referrals, longstanding relationships, and more business than you could possibly imagine. This, however, requires patience, and I admit that it's difficult for me to wait for the money to come (especially if you're just getting started). You have obligations to meet, employees to pay, and more, but you can afford to do what's right because—at the end of the day—the truth is free.

One last thing: Not only is the truth free, but it saves time. When you're honest, you spend time working on the right projects and contracts. When you're authentic and true to your strengths, your clients save time as they move on to contractors that are a better fit (or use your services and shorten the search).

AUTHENTICITY AS A SKILL

When we enter the workforce, we often assume that our 'skills' are tangible activities that everyone can see: copywriting, graphic design, leadership, degree-focused knowledge, etc. We build up these skills and fill our resumes to both impress potential employers and share our accomplishments.

But, what of authenticity? Authenticity is a skill just as important as your degree or work experience. In fact, authenticity is a skill you can employ at any time to enhance your already stellar reputation and image.

Authenticity brings a bit of humanity to the business world that your degree, your work experience, etc., cannot. The truth, reliability, authentic communication, and more show those around you that you know how to present yourself to the world as a genuine person and worker.

Yes, you may be a wonderful human being, but are you presenting that to the world? That level of authenticity is a skill that requires quite a bit of discernment.

You must be honest with yourself.

Ask yourself the following questions:
- How do I show the world that I'm an authentic personality?
- How do I live out the idea of reliability?
- Do I appear to be reliable to those around me?
- How do I live in and with the truth?
- Do my peers view me as trustworthy?

You may find that, when asking yourself these questions, it's difficult for those around you to see these attributes. Your peers, colleagues, friends, and family aren't mind readers. At times, our gifts are hidden, and while you don't want to be flashy and call attention to yourself, "look at me, I'm such a conscientious worker," you also don't want to sit so far back in the shadows that no one can see what you do.

For the sports fans reading this, these are attributes that don't show up on a stat sheet.

So, how do you make it clear to those around you that you live an authentic life and work with that same level of authenticity?

1) Actions speak louder than words. Say you'll do it and follow through.

2) Put yourself in your client's, customer's, colleague's, employee's shoes before acting.

   ...and

3) Always behave as if you plan to maintain the relationship for several decades.

DON'T SQUASH YOUR GIFTS

Finally, you must learn to live with the level of expertise you have attained. There's a time to speak up and a time to stand down. Famously, the military often asks us to, 'Lead, Follow, or Get Out of the Way.' There are moments when you can lead. At times, you must follow. There are also occasions when it's best to get out of the way. There's nothing wrong with staying in your lane, as it were.

Put another way, a therapist or preacher might ask you: "Do you want to be right? Or do you want to be in relationship?"

Thus, you must use quite a bit of discernment in your attempts to remain authentic. Yes, you want to (as we all do) remain trustworthy and provide the best services or goods to our customers. However, staying true to yourself means that there are times when you just don't have the answers.

Perhaps you've heard the ill-advised phrase 'the customer is always right.' Did you know this quip should end with…'in matters of taste?'

With this idea in mind, you can use your discernment to allow taste to rule the day. There's quite a big difference between, "Sir, I cannot allow you to post 27 guards at the front desk," and, "Sir, I understand your concerns about personal safety. We're happy to post a guard inside and outside the entryway to further ensure the safety of your employees and guests."

In one instance, you must act as the expert and give the client the specific advice you know they need. You're being true to yourself—you know better, and that's a good thing for your client.

On the other hand, a client who has (for example) been robbed or mugged in the past needs that extra bit of assurance, and creating a more robust security plan for them serves everyone quite well. No need to argue over one extra guard that, in the long run, is likely a good idea in today's world.

As your team bounces around ideas, there's a difference between, "I wouldn't quite put it that way," and "Because I wouldn't say it like that, it's wrong."

You can be true to yourself by stepping back and admitting any of the following things:
- I don't know
- I never thought of it that way before
- If that's what you want, I understand

- This isn't my area of expertise
- This is why we hire experts in this field
- I could be wrong
- I <u>was</u> wrong

Authenticity, then, isn't the simple act of remaining who you are on the face of it all at every moment of the day. You must also be the version of yourself that's required for the situation.

If you don't need to make the decisions, you can stand back. If the buck needs to stop with you—stop it. But every interaction is different. You can never approach every situation in exactly the same manner.

Those who choose to charge forward, take over every situation, or who lack discernment are effectively squashing their gifts. No one gets to see what you know because the clatter is always so loud. Authenticity requires you to ask questions, allow the experts to speak up, make decisions when necessary, search for answers, and make snap decisions. If you're willing to do all these things in due course, the world gets to see the whole of who you truly are. Otherwise, the commotion is too much for those who cannot bear to listen (or you're quiet as a church mouse and never heard).

LIVING AUTHENTICALLY

How does one go about the act of living authentically? I can't give you that answer. Your life, your job, your faith, your family: they all require varying degrees of authenticity presented in different ways. All I can tell you is that you must work diligently to remain authentic in all things at all times.

It's a task you must complete daily, and while it will become like second nature to you, there's no substitute for humility, grace, and compassion in the workplace and in your life, where authenticity is the most welcome of all attributes.

About James

James Radford, an esteemed business expert and visionary, conceived the idea of his own consultancy company back in 2015, laying the foundation for what would become the illustrious Trust Consulting Company. With unwavering determination and a keen eye for opportunities, James has propelled his company to unparalleled success in recent years, firmly establishing himself as a true titan of the business world. By establishing a successful business platform himself, James was able to crack the secrets of entrepreneurship and wants to spread the word.

Now, with a burning desire to make a profound impact on the lives of others, James is venturing into the realm of motivational speaking. Drawing from his wealth of experiences and hard-won wisdom, he aspires to guide those who find themselves trapped in life's struggles and empower aspiring entrepreneurs to realize their dreams. He believes in hard work and persistence above all else, and urges people that they can achieve their wildest dreams if they dare to work on them.

James's debut book, *This Can't Be It! – How To Not Let Circumstances Write Your Story*, delves into his own intricate battles with racism, illness, challenging relationships, and the profound significance of spirituality. The book will be available for pre-orders soon and aims to divulge the key factors that make a successful life.

Recognized for his expertise and accomplishments, James has graced prestigious platforms such as ABC, captivating audiences with his remarkable insights and compelling narratives. Armed with a dynamic presence and an unwavering commitment to making a difference, James Radford is poised to make waves in the world of entrepreneurship and leave an indelible mark on the lives of those he touches.

In addition to his remarkable professional journey, James Radford is also a devoted family man, cherishing the moments he spends with his beloved wife and children. Recognizing the importance of a strong and loving family unit, James actively contributes to their lives and plays an invaluable role

in shaping their growth and happiness. Whether it's sharing laughter, creating lasting memories, or offering unwavering support, James remains a steadfast presence in the lives of his wife and children, embracing the joys and challenges of family life with boundless
love and dedication.

For more information, visit:

- https://jwradford.com/

CHAPTER 7

BECOME FREE BY REPLACING YOURSELF

BY MIKE HECKMAN

Joe's Half Hour of Freedom:

Over the last decade I've come to realize that I get my joy from uncovering unexpected ways that I help the people I work with. Joe owns a successful construction business with four full time contractors. Joe called me from his cell, we were working on setting up a meeting during a week that I had very few openings. I offered to start my day earlier than usual on a Wednesday and Joe responded with, "I can't do any mornings." There was a quiver in his voice which made me immediately question why such emotion in his response.

Trying to understand I answered back with, "What do you mean, you can't do any mornings?"

Joe said, "I can't even take my daughter to school."

A bit flabbergasted, I asked, "Joe, what's up with that?"

He said, "I have to set up for the day."

I still didn't get it, so I just repeated, "...setup for the day?" As I repeated what he said as a question, I grabbed my legal pad and just listened. He described the materials that he made sure were on site, the equipment to be used, and the assignment of initial tasks for each of his guys. When he was finished, my notes for his routine filled up the top half of the first page of my legal pad.

"Joe, What I'm hearing is…" Then I read off my notes detailing his morning routine. "Who on your team can you count on to take care of this?"

Joe's first Standard Operating Procedure (SOP) was not a complex book written by two attorneys and an HR Manager. Instead, it was the top half-page of a legal pad crafted after a half-hour conversation.

Joe has good, long-term relationships with his team. Joe has leadership skills and was not afraid to delegate, his style was just to delegate in real time. His delegation style is face to face, with immediate personal feedback. Joe did not completely replace himself in his owner / manager position. Joe did get a precious extra half hour every morning of freedom by replacing himself each morning with a simple written morning check-list, and a little delegation. Joe now gets time with his daughter every morning as he takes her to school. I get so much joy being part of big impacts with such small changes, like Joe's half page SOP.

BECOME FREE BY REPLACING YOURSELF

In a world where entrepreneurs are celebrated for their drive, determination, and hands-on approach to building their businesses, the idea of becoming replaceable may seem counterintuitive. After all, isn't the goal of starting a business to be the one in charge, making all the important decisions and reaping the rewards of your hard work?

Most of us business owners have worked for someone at some

point in our lives. As an employee, we strive to make ourselves irreplaceable. We improve our value to the company and our income by having a unique set of skills or being the center of communication hubs. No one wants to buy a job. Instead, a potential buyer of your company wants to purchase a revenue stream that is as little work as possible.

While there's certainly something to be said for being the master of your own destiny, the truth is that building a successful business requires more than just a strong sense of leadership. It requires a willingness to delegate, to trust others, and to create systems and processes that allow your company to run smoothly even when you're not there.

I ask you to consider that becoming replaceable can be a key factor in adding value to your business. There are inherent benefits of delegating tasks, creating systems, and empowering your employees and we'll provide practical tips and strategies for how you can begin to implement these changes in your own business.

THE VALUE OF DELEGATION

As a business owner, it's easy to fall into the trap of thinking that you're the only one who can do certain tasks. After all, you built the business from the ground up, and you know it better than anyone else. But the truth is that if you're the only one doing everything, you're limiting your company's growth potential.

Delegating tasks to others not only frees up your own time and energy, but it also allows others to bring their own skills and expertise to the table. This can lead to new ideas and perspectives that can help your business grow and evolve in ways you never thought possible.

For example, imagine you're the owner of a small retail store. You're responsible for everything from ordering inventory to managing the sales floor to handling payroll. But by delegating some of these tasks to others, you can free up your own time to focus on big-picture strategy and growth initiatives.

You might hire a bookkeeper to oversee your finances, a sales manager to oversee the sales floor, and a part-time employee to help with inventory management. By doing so, you've not only lightened your own workload, but you've also created opportunities for others to contribute to the success of your business.

CREATING SYSTEMS AND PROCESSES

Delegating tasks is just one piece of the puzzle when it comes to becoming replaceable. Another key factor is creating systems and processes that allow your business to run smoothly, even when you're not there.

This might include things like creating a manual or handbook that outlines your company's policies and procedures, or implementing software that streamlines your workflow and automates certain tasks.

Standard Operating Procedures, or SOPs, are an essential part of any organization's operational framework. They play a crucial role in ensuring consistency, quality, and safety in the workplace. However, many employees view SOPs as dry, tedious documents that are difficult to understand and follow. In this chapter, we'll explore some strategies for making SOPs more accessible and engaging to employees, so they can be implemented effectively.

1. Keep it concise and clear

One of the primary reasons employees find SOPs difficult to follow is that they are often written in dense, technical language that can be hard to understand. To make SOPs more accessible and engaging, it's essential to keep them concise and clear. Use plain language and avoid jargon whenever possible. Break the information down into manageable sections with clear headings, bullet points, and diagrams, so it's easier for employees to digest.

2. Make it interactive

Another way to make SOPs more engaging is to create interactive elements that encourage employee participation. For example, you could create quizzes or interactive training modules that evaluate employees' knowledge of the SOPs. You could also create visual aids such as videos or infographics that illustrate the key points of the SOPs in a more engaging format.

3. Provide context

Employees are more likely to engage with SOPs if they understand why they are important and how they fit into the larger picture of the organization's goals. Provide context for the SOPs by explaining how they support the organization's mission and values. Highlight the benefits of following the SOPs, such as increased efficiency, improved quality, and reduced risk.

4. Involve employees in the development process

When employees participate in the development process of SOPs, they are more likely to take ownership of them and feel invested in their success. Solicit feedback from employees on the clarity and usefulness of the SOPs and make revisions based on their input. You could also involve employees in the creation of training materials or other interactive elements to make the SOPs more engaging.

SOPs are a crucial component of any organization's operations, but they don't have to be dry and tedious documents that employees dread. By following these strategies for making SOPs more accessible and engaging, you can ensure that your employees are equipped to follow the procedures effectively, leading to improved quality, consistency, and safety in the workplace.

For example: if you're the owner of a small marketing agency, you might create a system for onboarding new clients that includes a checklist of tasks to be completed, such as setting up a project management tool, scheduling a kickoff call, and assigning team members to specific tasks.

By creating a system like this, you're not only ensuring that all necessary tasks are completed in a timely manner, but you're also empowering your team to take ownership of the process and make improvements where necessary.

EMPOWERING YOUR EMPLOYEES

A key aspect of becoming replaceable is empowering your employees to take on more responsibility and make decisions on their own. This not only frees up your own time, but it also helps to create a sense of ownership and investment among your team members.

One way to empower your employees is to provide them with the necessary training and resources.

TRAINING AND RESOURCES

In my experience, for your employees to take on more responsibility and make decisions on their own, they need to have the necessary training and resources at their disposal. This might include access to training materials, mentorship programs, or even funding for continuing education.

For example: if you're the owner of a Financial Services or Information Technology company, you might provide your employees with access to online training courses or send them to industry conferences to learn about the latest trends and technologies.

By investing in your employees' growth and development, you're not only helping them to become more knowledgeable and skilled, but you're also building a team that is capable of taking on more responsibility and contributing to the success of your business.

THE BENEFITS OF BECOMING REPLACEABLE

So why should you strive to become replaceable in your own business? Here are just a few of the benefits:

1. Freedom and Flexibility

When you're the only one running your business, everything falls on your shoulders. But by delegating tasks, creating systems, and empowering your employees, you can free up your own time and create more flexibility in your schedule.

This might mean taking a much-needed vacation without worrying about your business falling apart in your absence, or simply having more time to focus on your own personal interests and hobbies.

2. Scalability

If your business is solely dependent on you, it's difficult to scale and grow beyond a certain point. But by becoming replaceable, you're creating a structure that can support growth and expansion.

This might mean expanding your team, branching out into new product lines or services, or even exploring opportunities for franchising or licensing your business model.

3. Increased Value

A business that is dependent on its owner is not as valuable as one that has a strong team and systems in place. By becoming replaceable, you're increasing the value of your business and making it more attractive to potential buyers or investors.

4. Peace of Mind

Finally, becoming replaceable can provide peace of mind. Knowing that your business can run smoothly without you can alleviate stress and anxiety and allow you to focus on the things that matter most to you.

PRACTICAL TIPS FOR BECOMING REPLACEABLE

If you're ready to start building a business that can run without you, here are some practical tips to help you get started:

1. Start small.

Delegating tasks and creating systems can be overwhelming at first. Start by delegating just one task or creating a system for one process and build from there.

2. Hire the right people.

When hiring employees or contractors, look for those who are initiative-taking, responsible, and have a strong work ethic. These are the people who will be able to take on more responsibility and help your business grow.

3. Communicate clearly.

Make sure that everyone on your team understands their roles and responsibilities, and that they have the necessary resources and support to do their jobs effectively.

4. Invest in training and development.

Provide your employees with the necessary training and resources to help them grow and develop in their roles. This will not only benefit your business, but it will also help to build loyalty and trust among your team members.

5. Embrace technology.

Look for opportunities to automate tasks and streamline processes using software or other tools. This can help to free up your own time and create a more efficient and effective business.

There are inherent benefits of delegating tasks, creating systems, and empowering your employees. As you progress to becoming more replaceable, you are not only helping add enterprise value to your business, but you are moving toward more personal freedom and better life balance.

About Mike

Mike Heckman is a nationally-recognized Financial Educator, Author, Podcaster, Speaker, Retirement Planner, and Wealth Advisor.

Mike has been helping business owners, medical professionals, and retirees preserve, protect, and pass on their wealth since 2009. In 2019 Mike founded Sable Point Wealth Management with Michigan office locations in Ludington and Spring Lake.

Mike is currently conducting dissertation research on wealth preservation strategies in retirement to complete his Financial Management Doctorate from California Southern University.

Mike's completed education includes a Master of Science Degree in Financial Planning, including coursework on Behavioral Finance, and a Bachelor of Business Administration in which he studied Business Management and Computer Information Systems. In 2021, Mike earned the Certificate in Blockchain and Digital Assets® from the Digital Assets Council of Financial Professionals and New York Institute of Finance. Mike has been a CERTIFIED FINANCIAL PLANNER™ practitioner since 2014.

Mike believes that people make better decisions when they align their goals, values, and actions. Financial advisors who invest in their own education achieve better outcomes for their clients.

Qualifications:
- CFP® CERTIFIED FINANCIAL PLANNER
- CERTIFIED VALUE BUILDER™ ADVISOR
- CEPA® CERTIFIED EXIT PLANNING ADVISOR
- BFA™ BEHAVIORAL FINANCIAL ADVISOR
- CDFA® CERTIFIED DIVORCE FINANCIAL ANALYST
- AWMA® ACCREDITED WEALTH MANAGEMENT ADVISOR
- SE-AWMA® SPORTS & ENTERTAINMENT WEALTH MANAGEMENT ADVISOR
- CPRC® CHARTERED RETIREMENT PLANNING COUNSELOR
- CPRS® CHARTERED RETIREMENT PLANS SPECIALIST

Contact Mike at:

- Website: www.sablepointwealthmanagement.com
- Podcast: The Wealth Dock Podcast www.wealthdock.com

CHAPTER 8

THE IMPOSSIBLE DREAMS

BY PAUL P. PHIMASONE

On a Tuesday evening, I was born in Vientiane, (Capital City of LAO PDR). My mother's name is Lanoi, and my father's name is Phouvong.

I remember that since I was 3 years old, I would sit in the back of a Solex Scooter. It is a motorized bicycle that was quite popular in France in the 20th Century, which made me marvel at the engineering behind it.

At the age of 7, I learned about entrepreneurship by collecting empty discarded glass bottles and selling them to local street vendors who would come ringing the bell in front of our house.

Learning is a treasure that will follow its owner everywhere.
~ Chinese Proverb

The same year, our whole family, including me, a total of 7 people, moved to Saigon (Ho Chi Minh City), Vietnam from 1957 to 1960. My dad represented Laos as an Ambassador. That's where I learned how to speak Vietnamese at home and at Jean-Jacques Rousseau High School. I had a chance to see the Vietnamese President Ngo Dinh Diem when he was invited to the reception at our Embassy home.

I always believed in free enterprise – since I was a teenager. My brother Pascal (Khoun's Laotian Name) is informed whenever I have a new project to announce. He is like a Vice President of the Company. In one earlier entrepreneurial venture, I built a radio tube amplifier and sold it to a musician friend in March 1971 before I came to the USA.

According to statistics. It takes 21 days to form a new habit before a new one is formed.

> *The heart of a fool is in his mouth, but the mouth of a wise man is in his heart.*
> ~ Benjamin Franklin

Challenge #1: Set your dreams high and go after them. Don't let anybody talk you out of your vision to accomplish your goal. Two quotes that elaborate on this concept are:

> *People don't care how much you know until they know how much you care.*
> ~ Pres. Theodore Roosevelt

> *Even if you are on the right track, you will get run over if you just sit there.*
> ~ Will Rogers

Adaptation: My first enterprise was buying and selling PC computers back in the '80s. I didn't even know how to operate a computer, but that did not deter me and cause me to give up. After I was criticized by one of my close friends, I started learning on my own how to operate MS-DOS (Microsoft Disk Operating System) and all the components. I learned by reading and practicing, even taking a computer apart. (The purchase price was $1500 – made by Canon Computers.)

Challenge #2: Now stress is building up because you're standing out of the crowd. Have you heard people laughing at you at work, or on social media, or even your own brothers, sisters, or relatives saying you'll never amount to anything? We've all heard those comments over and over again.

I also remember someone saying, "I am going to be the last person standing in line laughing all the way to the Bank."

Adaptation: Even with trial and error, sometimes the PC Computer I was building kept crashing. Finally, I sold one desk top computer to the friend of a friend. I am feeling like I landed on the moon—and the rest is history.

A journey of thousand miles begins with a single step.
~ Chinese Proverb

Challenge #3: You need wisdom. It was King Solomon, the wisest man who ever lived, who expressed it so well:

For Wisdom is better than rubies; and all the things that may be desired are not to be compared to it.
~ Wise Sayings of Solomon, Proverbs 8:11 KJV

Give instruction to a wise man, and he will be yet wiser: teach a just man, and he will increase in learning.
~ Wise Sayings of Solomon, Proverbs 9:9 KJV

Learn as much as you can; take online courses in your field of interest. For example, YouTube channels offer a tremendous amount of education on just about any subject.

The only thing worse than being blind is having sight but no vision. We can do anything we want to if we stick to it long enough.
~ Helen Keller

Adaptation: A few years later, I went out (driving from Alexandria, Virginia to Washington, DC) to put an ad in the

Washington Post for a week since I couldn't afford two or more weeks of advertising.

Challenge #4: You have to have courage to succeed regardless of the economy or country you belong to. There is always a solution if you are willing to chase the rainbow – pay the price and go for it.

> *The accumulation of small advantages that added up to long-term victory.*
> ~ Sun Tzu, the great Chinese General

Adaptation: In pursuing my dream, I sometimes wondered if I was doing the right thing. However, I got a two calls, one from a gentleman from Georgetown University Medical School (a Brain Surgeon) and another from a State Police Officer, asking me to put computers together for them to purchase. It was an exciting opportunity to keep working.

Challenge #5: You have to have Integrity, as quoted by Warren Buffett, which reminds us that we must possess it within ourselves. Otherwise, you can't make it big in the real world.

Adaptation: In some cases, if a customer changes their plan, for the sake of integrity I offer them reimbursement.

Challenge #6: You have to have Honesty, (per Sam Walton ¬– Founder of Wal-Mart), in yourself and with others. This may mean you have to swim against the current, communicate and be positive.

Adaptation: The customers is always right if they have an issue with your products.

Challenge #7: You need to have commitment to pursue a good work ethic.

> *Do not wait for leaders; do it alone, person to person. It is not how we do, but how much love we put in the doing.*
> ~ Mother Theresa

Adaptation: The best way to react is to change friends or jobs. Most people think if they have a kind or perfect boss, or even a custom home, everything is just fine. Many of us don't think we should be changing ourselves. So we resist change, we fight for everything, and complain about everything – such as the government, the country, the county, etc. Here in the USA, we take so many things for granted.

Challenge #8: You need to have the ability to conquer fear. The best way to conquer fear is to take action. We also have to guard against taking on more than we can handle. This reminds us of Theologian Desmond Tutu's statement: "How do we eat an elephant? One piece at a time."

In addition, in today's modern world, everybody wants instant everything – like a Microwave Oven.

> *The hunger for love is much more difficult to remove than the hunger for bread.*
> ~ Mother Theresa

Adaptation: Successful individuals are constantly changing and adapting to new circumstances because of their mindset or habit of doing things, which unsuccessful people are not willing to do.

Challenge #9: Find ways to laugh as often as you can. Remember the old saying: "Laughter is the best medicine." Laughter keeps you young.

> *Humor is an affirmation of your dignity. It shows you are bigger than all your challenges.*
> ~ Anonymous

Adaptation: Smell the roses along the way. Be frugal but treat yourselves every now and then. Remember the saying : Love yourself so you can love others.

Challenge #10: You must have the ability to have fun.

Peace begins with a smile
~ Mother Theresa

He who thinks too much about every step he takes
will always stay in one leg.
~ Chinese Proverb

Adaptation: Everything is changing rapidly including your body. (Not to mention your customers, clients, friends and relatives too.)

Challenge #11: Learn from everybody – from Animals to Children and Elderly People.

A book holds a house of gold. Learning is a weightless treasure
you can carry easily.
~ Chinese Proverb

Adaptation: Take a break every now and then, go out into fresh air. Get more sunlight to help boost the Vitamin D the body needs. Eat healthy food, vegetables and fruit to nourish your soul. And of course, do some exercises or Yoga or whatever you can – just keep moving and moving.

Challenge #12: Don't put other people down because they are poor, someday they may be richer than you can imagine.

When you see a tree fall, you can walk across the branch. When
you see a human fall, don't walk across them.
~ Laotian Proverb

Adaptation: A small branch is easy to bend and adjust. But when it grows tall, it is hard to bend.
Same for human beings. At an early age, children are easy to teach. When their grow up, it is hard to teach them a good manner or any new value in life.

Challenge #13: With today's technology, we have many ways to communicate. Stay up to date on using the devices or equipment. This is like a vehicle that can move from point A to B faster than in any other period in human history.

Challenge #14: Don't be afraid to ask for help, especially when internal problems arise faster than you can participate. Quitters never win, winners never quit.

A slip of the foot you may soon recover, but a slip of the tongue you may never get over.
~ Benjamin Franklin

Challenge #15: Accept the responsibility of your own action, whether it's a success or a failure. Your failures can be your best teachers.

The world breaks everyone, and afterward some are strong at the broken places.
~ Ernest Hemingway

Challenge #16: Find the good in everybody. The more fun you have with people, the more you're going learn from them or from each other.

Challenge #17: Learn to be flexible. Be adaptable to unfamiliar territory and any situation you find yourself in.

As my dad quotes:

When you join the black bird, you change and adapt like the black bird.

When you join the white bird, you do the same as white bird.
~ Phouvong Phimmasone

This lesson has served me well since I came and grew up here in the USA.

Challenge #18: Learn to get along with everybody, including your competitors. Pray for them even if they give you a hard time.

Challenge #19: Turn your enemy into energy to succeed in your favor. I can give you many examples, in case after case. "It is not the sign of the fight; it is the ability to hang in there when things get tough."

Adaptation: I remember one time, back in the '90s, when I was standing at a government sales event for used equipment and computers, there was a fellow who would always beat me there to get ahead; we had an argument but the problem was resolved, and today we have become friends; now, he is always on the look out to give me more computers for recycling.

Challenge #20: Never, ever give up. "When things get tough, the tough is get going."

Never give in. Never give in. Never, never, never, never—in nothing, great on small, large or petty—never give in, except to convictions of honour and good sense.
~ Winston Churchill

His words emphasize the importance of persistence, determination, and standing firm in face of challenges and adversity.

Adaptation: In another scenario, someone recommended that I explore alternative ways to sell to consumers through online platforms. As a result, I met many friends who ultimately led me to co-author this book.

Challenge #21: Keep reviewing your success and failures. As many successful speakers and leaders have often said: There is no great failure, only a great lesson. An interviewer once asked Thomas Edison, You failed 1800 times to build a light bulb and you are not giving up? Mr. Edison said: "I have not failed, I found 1800 ways not to build a light bulb."

Adaptation: In conclusion, we can't judge the book by its cover, nor would we put others down because of their race, ethnicity, or religious background. We all are children of God.

I wish all readers the very best and successful endeavors in the years to come, so we can celebrate many more years and set an example for the next generation.

The hardest paths lead to most beautiful destinations. Dare to take that path, you will never be the same. Keep going! Your hardest times often lead to the greatest moments of your life.
~ Lao Tzu

About Paul

Paul P. Phimasone is an Asian-American born in Laos, a landlocked country in Southeast Asia. He is an accomplished tech entrepreneur with over two decades of experience in the software and hardware industries. As a young man, he and his classmate built a Radio AM Broadcasting station, named "Radio 1966," from old radio tubes and electronics salvage parts.

Paul began teaching himself at an early age, inventing an intercom using a strand of tiny wire connecting two speakers without the need of batteries. He also built a small rocket using discarded aluminum tubes and black powders, as well as an airplane propeller out of a carved 2 by 4 of lighter wood.

> *You can't solve a problem with the same mind that created it.*
> ~ Albert Einstein

He has a passion for learning new things and spends dedicated time on accomplishing projects and helping others succeed. He contributes a lifelong lesson from his dad: "Persistence, passion, and never give up. Act as if it is already done in every encounter, no matter the difficulties that arise, and remain positive at all times."

> *All our dreams come true if we have the courage to pursue them.*
> ~ Walt Disney

When he is not working, he enjoys walking or swimming, listening to epic music, as well as tending to his exotic plants and herbs while on his knees in his garden. Paul speaks five languages.

Contact Paul at:

- paulpphimasone.com

CHAPTER 9

BEYOND THE BOX
DISRUPT. IMPACT. INSPIRE.

BY BABLY BHASIN

If you always do what you've always done, you'll always be where you've always been.
~ James Emery White

Here's to the mindful ones, the forward thinkers, the visionaries.
The ones who don't want to live life just as it is. Who want more. Who provoke better.
The bold, who dare to create a better reality. The ones who choose to make it happen.
Making decisions that lead forward. To leave a legacy that will make our children proud.
Because these are the changemakers. And while some may see them as far out,
I see legends. The ones who do give a damn.

Out came a charming, blue-eyed, handsome young boy, with the words "I'm a Little Samurai" printed in bold white letters against the orange and black striped background of his bandana. Clear skin, rosy-pink cheeks, and a big, beautiful, blooming smile adorned his face as his father wheeled him out of the doctor's office.

SUCCESS IN ANY ECONOMY

The song, *Happy*, by Pharrell Williams...

"Clap along if you feel like happiness is the truth,
 Clap along if you know what happiness is to you,
 Clap along if you feel like that's what you wanna do"

...radiated from his headphones, onto the people sitting in the cancer care clinic.

My husband walked up to him, feeling the urge to become acquainted, and said, "Hey there, little samurai! I love your bandana. And, that's my favorite song too. Sorry to startle you but I couldn't resist saying hi! May I have the honor of knowing your name?"

"My name is Akio. My dad says it means I'm a hero," he said. "I'm eight years old. I'm little right now but when I grow up, I will be a strong samurai just like Miyamoto Musahi. I will take care of everyone and fight all the bad guys with my sword."

With confidence and clarity, he continued, "Sometimes, I get tired, but then I talk to my brain, to give me more power, and it does. I also love to paint and write, just like Miyamoto. I will make my mama and papa proud of me one day."

All seventy of us, in the room, had our ears tuned in to Akio's words. There was something powerful about this little boy that made you want to hear him, root for him, remember him. An old man stood up slowly from the audience and gave Akio a salute. Within seconds, like a domino effect, everyone stood up and did the same. Oh boy! Akio was gleaming with pride. This little chap was, undoubtedly, destined to make a mark.

Suddenly Akio's mother, who was standing behind her son and husband, fell crumbling down to her knees. Her eyes were swollen and full of unshed tears, and a silence that couldn't be held within her any longer.

She blurted in a whisper, "One week. The doctor said Akio has only one week left."

No one heard her murmuring emotions except me, as I was standing closest to her. I picked her up, my lips unable to find words. All I could muster was a long, heartful, speechless, "I see you / I hear you / I feel you" hug.

(Pause...If you knew you were going to die in one week, how differently would you have created your legacy?)

Nothing makes you realize that life is truly a privilege received more than death. You owe yourself the courage and the integrity to be the best possible version of you. And, if you ever feel confused or lost in life, go and spend two weeks in the cancer ward. Clarity will kick in faster than a bullet train, into all areas of your life.

By this time in life, it had become quite clear that the universe was trying to tell me something, giving me clues to decipher my life-puzzle. "Nothing in your life is happening by accident. Go into the depth of your soul and understand who you truly are. Then shall you find your greatness." Intuitively, I knew I was going through all this for a reason, a higher purpose, something beyond the box.

As I stood shoulder-to-shoulder with children, wives, and husbands just like us, I became even more cognizant of my purpose. In the chaos and unity of cancer, my husband and I founded *Sameza*. It is our battle against cancer, against diabetes, against the status quo.

I envision a cancer-free world in which the vast majority of people can live their dreams, feel health-safe and return home to be with their families; where businesses take a stand for integrity with empathy, and we 'together-as-one' support each other to make it happen. I believe we are here to create history, not repeat it. And, I am looking for as many people as possible who will join me in this cause.

Why?

...Because, enough is enough.
...Because, we deserve better.
...Because, our children deserve better.
...Because, it's absolutely, beyond any doubt, imperative.
...Because, I do give a damn.

And whilst Akio still lingered in my mind, so did another gentleman, Gulzar Saab – the most renowned and enthralling poet of India. During an interview, the host asked, "How do you write with such unbelievable imagery and profundity, that it touches the heart of every soul who reads it? Does one need to go through pain, so as to communicate with such depth?"

"I have not gone through as much pain in my life as many others. It's really not necessary that your heart has to break, to feel the intensity of an emotion. But certainly, one has to have or develop a high level of *awareness, emotional intelligence and empathy* to emote. Thereafter, it emanates naturally from within, into all areas of your life," replied Gulzarji, in his graceful demeanor. Simply put, the higher your awareness, the higher your empathy, the higher your compassion, the higher your emotional intelligence. Fortunately, empathy is not a fixed trait, it can be learned.

And isn't this what our world needs more of? I believe being a leader is more than just wanting to lead, it's an authentic expression of oneself. Leadership is about empathy; it is about audacious torch-bearers, compassionate and courageous to take humanity forward, who think in generations to create higher standards that will become the new normal of the future. As Steve Jobs said, "Innovation distinguishes between a leader and a follower." We cannot create a better world with status quo mentalities, expectations and finite outcomes. The prerequisites of a better future are empathy, integrity, innovative thinking and disruption. The future will belong to those who dare to disrupt things today.

No Guts, No Glory! No Legend, No Story!

On Sept 30, 2017, just like Akio's mom, I found myself crumbled down to my knees, on the balcony of my house. The clouds were black and the winds cold, the rain bucketing down like sheets on me. I was amidst the biggest tsunami of my life. Silence, screams, tears, fears, anger, and so much more, all clenched within me. I had just completed the last rites of my dear husband, with my three little girls.

"Where do I go from here on? How do I move forward? What do you want from me, universe?" I asked, in the downbursts of rain. "Why didn't you take me, instead of my husband, dear God? Why have you kept me alive?" I was desperately trying to find answers; unable to make sense of the things that were befalling my life. Like a jumping CD player, my life's movie was rewinding and replaying, over and over again, in my mind. Yet, even in the clouds of exhaustion, there was one thing I knew for sure...I wasn't given this blessing of a life just to die paying bills. There's no way in hell that my existence could be so meagre and irrelevant. I wasn't born to be mediocre. I was born to make a dent in the universe. If there was one defining moment, in which I can say my hunger was on fire, this was it.

"Get back up Bably. Hold your head up high, ignite your fire, and walk your greatness," commanded my soul.

That night, I decided, I will be unstoppable.

As you have probably guessed by now, I love playing the game of possibility versus the game of probability. Or, as Simon Sinek would say, the infinite versus the finite game. *Possibility is soul power*. It's an unwavering belief stating, "I know who I am. I know where I want to go. I know why I want to get there. And, that's all I need to know. Period." On the other hand, probability is a "maybe" that keeps you caged in self-doubt, self-distrust and insecurity. You can either be a free flying eagle or a caged one. You always have a choice.

I knew where I wanted to go, I knew why I wanted to get there, but something inside me said, *"Who are you?* Get to know yourself deeper, way deeper." In order to disrupt things outside, you have to earnestly understand yourself. As Jay Samit states, "All disruption starts with introspection." Thus began my inner journey to the center of my soul, which was, surprisingly, extremely fun.

I believe our life, our story, is like a big jigsaw puzzle, waiting to be solved. "You can only connect the dots looking backwards," said Steve Jobs. Our vision, our purpose, our answers, all lie within us itself. One must have the courage to open their Pandora's box.

How about we do this exercise for fun: Let's begin with looking at 'your life' puzzle. Remember it as far back as you can. Every tab denotes a stage in life (childhood, youth, early adulthood, marriage, children, etc.). Zoom into one tab, one at a time, and you will find major life events within each of them. Now, zoom in further and you will uncover your personality or your 'technical personal details' – like traits, qualities, feelings, views, words, actions, attitude, etc. Your personality is who you are and what you do when everyone is watching. In corporate terms, this is the 'perceived value' of your brand.

Stay with me! Zoom in deeper and you will arrive to your character, your 'truest inner self'. It encompasses your principles, morals, beliefs, values, etc. Characteristics such as empathy, integrity, honesty, responsibility, compassion, contribution, justice, courage, leadership, loyalty, determination, etc., will be found here. Your character is who you are and what you do when nobody is watching. In corporate terms, this is the 'real value' of your brand.

Everything you are, say, and do, represents YOU. It's an authentic manifestation of who you are and what you believe. Just like you are the leader of your personal brand; a corporate leader is the brand ambassador of his/her business. Each of us has dreams, a story and a lifespan. Research indicates that deciphering the puzzle to its "real value" is the first act of an intentional leader. Businesses don't disrupt unless the individuals do. There are a few leaders who choose to disrupt-impact rather than manipulate in order to inspire others. Every single one of these inspiring leaders thinks, acts and communicates from the inside out, from character rather than personality. Consciously or not, they follow a pattern, one that I call *The Lion Code*.

The concept of *The Lion Code* was inspired by my hunger to understand myself. While there are many personality tests available (and very few character assessments), I found them to be quite fragmented and unsatisfying. They were not comprehensive and in-depth enough to satisfy my search. Therefore, I developed one myself. This alternative perspective is not just useful for self and outer awareness, but it's a practical application that has seen me and my clients through the most intense storms, roadblocks, and uncertainties in life (personal and corporate). It also allowed me to remain in control as I marched forward on my cause. It can be used as a guide to vastly improve clarity by understanding the real problem, give direction, and choose the relevant actions needed to move forward. And it all starts from the innermost core. It starts with the 'real value' character.

The Lion Code is a bullseye comprised of three concentric circles. Starting from the inside out: The innermost circle interprets mindset, honesty, courage and integrity. The next circle clarifies perceptions, values, beliefs and what you choose to take a stand for. The outermost circle deals with dreams, passion, trust, sincerity, grit, determination, etc. In my upcoming book, *The Lion Code*, the bullseye is a thorough 'R.E.A.L. Value' analysis that can help you reveal your truest authenticity and re-ignite your inner lion, so that you too can manifest your greatness to the world and inspire millions with your voice.

Just like you, I am on a timeline. We only get one life, and there are no dress rehearsals. The curtain is up, and the world awaits to experience your greatness. *So light up your lion, coz its showtime!*

My life is finite, but life is infinite. To live a life with the disrupt-impact-inspire ethos means thinking about the generations ahead. The goal is to perpetuate beyond-the-box leaders who will pave the way for the next generation of leaders to come. No one wants on their tombstone only the dates of when we came and went. The greatest memory is the impact we made and the many lives we inspired along the way.

Lastly… "Whatever you do, always do it with character and integrity."

As Simon Sinek says:

A signpost stands at the fork in the road.
Pointing in one direction, the sign says 'Victory.'
Pointing in another direction, the sign says 'Fulfillment.'
You must pick a direction.
Which one will you choose?

About Bably

Bably Bhasin is a 'Making-An-Impact' Disruptive Entrepreneur who has earned her crown as Bestselling Author with multiple soul-inspiring books under her belt. As a contributing author in her first bestselling book, *MindStirring Business Secrets* - an anthology presented by Kevin Harrington, she asserts "The future belongs to those who will disrupt things today." Not only does she walk her talk, she walks the walk with en route winners to see them rise and shine. A trailblazing thought leader and an influential motivational speaker, she helps people discover their superpowers so that together we can impact our world and leave an impressive impressionable legacy for our next generations.

Bably is the Founder and CEO of Sameza Pte Ltd, the one and only makers of the one-and-only health-transforming rice in the world. Sameza is named after her three daughters: SA is Sana, which means hope; ME is Mehr, which means gratitude; ZA is Naweza, which means "I Can Do It." Launched in Singapore in 2016, Sameza is an award-winning, internationally acclaimed company that has been gaining sweeping recognition worldwide for its Harvard Medical School accredited, health-transforming superfood rice, Sameza Vintage Collection (SVC).

This artisan superfood was designed exclusively for The Royal Families with elite requirements of luxurious quality, taste, nutrition and health, and it is now available to the public. With prestigious awards like Great Taste and being named a 'Star Revelation' by Michelin Guide, Bhasin is making a global impact by revolutionizing the way people consume daily staples.

In 2015, Bably's husband was diagnosed with cancer. As she stood shoulder-to-shoulder with children, wives and husbands facing this dreadful disease, she realized the power of her rice. SVC was the regal superfood that helped her husband fight his cancer and it became a blessing for their fellow patients too. "OMG! If this can heal cancer patients, when the body is in its most critical state, imagine what it can do for everyone else." Sameza clearly represents her battle against cancer, diabetes, and the status quo. WHY? Because, we all deserve better. Because, every life matters.

In 2020, the company achieved a roaring victory on *The Virtual Shark Tank* hosted by the Original Shark, Mr. Kevin Harrington, and a standing ovation by the team and entire audience. Unequivocally, Bably is nothing short of a trailblazer. Besides being the only woman founder in her industry, this 'Rice Queen' has become a beacon of hope for millions of families.

She has been seen in *Michelin Guide, theAsianparent, Emperics Asia, The Wellness Insider, Food Navigator Asia, Clozette, Vanilla Luxury*, and has appeared on CNA938, MoneyFM89.3 and Ticker News across Asia.

With an impactful start in Singapore, Bably is now forging ahead into global markets to make her regal superfood accessible to millions worldwide. With honour she promotes her life motto: "Whatever you do, always do it with character and integrity."

To contact Bably:

- Learn more: www.sameza.com
- Get in touch: bably@sameza.com
- LinkedIn: linkedin.com/in/bably-bhasin-488197132

CHAPTER 10

TO THRIVE IN A DOWN ECONOMY, YOU MUST BE...YOU!

BY SHAWN MASON

In order to be your genuine self, you must first know yourself. I used to wonder how two people with similar backgrounds and similar experiences, like brothers from the same household, could end up being entirely different people. One could end up as a model citizen with a closely-knit family and successful work life, while the other goes from job to job, never having enough money and not being able to maintain lasting relationships, etc.

I believe that one of the differences is that the first brother took his experiences, both good and bad, and processed them. That sounds complicated, I know. But to process an event, even a traumatic one, is to simply give the event meaning. However, you must not only give it meaning but you must give it an empowering meaning. By giving our experiences, both good and bad, an empowering meaning, it gives us the ability to use them as a learning and launching experience.

When we learn from our experiences, we gain wisdom which we can use as a launching pad to move to the next level. I often hear people state that they don't think about the past because it is too painful or there is nothing to gain from it. This type of thinking is similar to paying for a key, but never walking through the door to access the treasure you just unlocked. The treasure sits there and rots. You refuse to claim it and no one else can benefit from it either. For others to benefit from it, you must first claim it. By claiming it, you can pass on this treasure of an experience.

Not all experiences are positive. In my own life, I have learned more from disappointment and failure than I would ever have learned from success. Failures made me step back and evaluate harder. I had to ask tough questions like:

- "Where did my thinking go wrong?"
- "Where did my attitude go wrong?"
- "What did I do to help precipitate this event?"
- "What steps can I take to prevent this from happening again?"
- "What can I learn from this?"
- ...and others.

I would ask disempowering questions like, "Why does this always happen to me?" or "Why are people so mean?" etc. These types of questions removed me from control and implied that I was a victim. *While in truth, the event may have happened to you and you bore the brunt of it, you cannot accept that you had zero part in it and you must never accept that you are a victim.* Victims are helpless. You are never helpless. You can learn, grow, and overcome...every...single...time.

Once you have profited from your experiences by processing them and gaining the wisdom they have to teach you, then you can use that knowledge to understand what you like and don't like, what you are good at and not good at, and what you flow in and don't flow in. These three ideas are closely related but do have distinctions. When you like something, you rarely pay attention to the time. You are 'in the moment' and doing what brings you joy. Sometimes hours can go by before you realize it.

This is closely related to 'flow' in that you are just 'doing'. No thought is required, and the expertise flows out of you without stress or pressure. This type of activity is also called unconscious competence. You are good at it without giving it a lot of effort or thought.

This activity is your genuine self. You are good at it, you enjoy it, and it requires little effort from you. To be successful in business, you need to know this about yourself and accept only the activities that meet this requirement. When you flow in an activity you like, then the minimal effort required leaves both physical time and emotional energy to do other things or even more of the same activity. Life is much more enjoyable when you are not getting the life sucked out of you by people and activities that you "feel" you have to do.

Never be afraid to be yourself. It is true that some people will not like you…at all. It is also true that some people will like you…no matter what. Kobe Bryant once said, "No matter what, people are going to like you or not like you. So be authentic and let them like you or not for who you actually are." It is okay for some people to not like you. If everyone likes everyone, then there might not be a lot of options and choices in the world. Everything would be boring and mundane. Being different, as long as it is not harmful to others, is probably the greatest gift you can give humanity. Show the world what it is to simply be true to who you are and perhaps give them the courage to do the same.

A person who knows who they are and what they want will never lack for work. There is a place and purpose for them. If the economy is strong, they will have work or a job. If the economy is down, they will have work or a job. St. Catherine of Siena said, "Be who you were created to be, and you will set the world on fire." Have you defined your ideal client or your ideal position? If not, then how will you be able to identify it when you come across it? How many lost opportunities have passed you by because you have not, in detail, created what the ideal client or position looks like?

To create what the ideal client or ideal position looks like requires you to know what you want and what you excel at. Often, what you excel at are those things that come easy to you or those things that when you are doing them, the time flies by. It is far easier to spot what you want when it is clear in your mind. We get what we focus on, and a clearly-defined client or position is something that can be focused on. Knowing what you want requires you to be your genuine self. You have to understand what you are good at, what you are not so good at, and what brings you joy.

Often doing activities that you are not good at requires mental discipline. Mental discipline requires emotional energy. Your emotional energy is like a battery. It can be charged to full and run for a good amount of time but eventually it needs to be recharged. If your business life tends to be full of battery-sucking activities, then you will run out of power to perform well. Knowing what drains you and what energizes you is of the utmost importance when it comes to defining your ideal client or position.

I have a friend who would constantly be shuffling through clients. He would replace them at an alarming rate. He was a very stressed person and had very little time to do much else other than work. He had a few employees who helped him with his clients, but it was never easy. He constantly worried about losing clients because he never said, "no". He never said "no" when taking a new client, he never fired a bad client, and he never refused to do what was being asked of him. He was so paranoid about not getting new clients that he was doing only mediocre work and would lose some clients because of that.

The best business advice I ever received was the statement, 'What you have obtained with talent should be maintained with integrity.' I have applied this to my own life in a myriad of ways and have often passed it on. When you focus on what you are good at, it is easy to win that business. Keeping it is another thing entirely. I gave my friend this advice through a long discussion over wine one night, and he took it to heart. He even did what

I did with it, he wrote it down on a post-it note and attached it under his computer monitor to remind him every day, all day. For him, integrity spoke to his ideal client.

I recall the day he began talking about exactly what his ideal client would look like. He had decided that only those who fit his ideal model would become his new clients. A few months down the road I noticed he was a bit more relaxed. A little more time passed, and he was earning 2 to 3 times what he previously was. When asked about it, he explained it this way: By only accepting clients that were his ideal, he was able to focus on the processes needed to satisfy those subsets of clients. He became better at tasks and his tasks produced better and better results. His clients were happy and did not mind paying a little more for excellent work. And suddenly, he was able to serve more clients and serve them better. His income displayed this newfound work strategy.

In a down economy, he was tempted to betray his ideal client but was encouraged by his life coach not to do so. With a bit of trepidation, he kept true to himself and was never short of solid-paying clients. In fact, when the economy took a downturn, his business thrived. His income actually went up during a downturn. Why? Because he took the time to learn what he wanted and what he was good at. Then he clarified his ideal client and did not compromise. His results speak for themselves.

Matthew McConaughey stated, "Knowing who we are is hard. Eliminate who we're not first, and we'll find ourselves where we need to be."

There is wisdom in the idea of eliminating everything that is not...us. When you remove the noise from your life, you may find that the music you can now hear is more beautiful than you could ever have imagined...the music of who you are. Your song is unique in all the world. There is no other "you". There is only you, and if you are not you, then no one else will be there to show the world what kind of music you are.

The privilege of a life is being who you are.
~ Joseph Campbell

Learn who you are and let the world see it. "What's that? A downturned economy? I'm sorry I cannot hear it because the music of my purpose is too loud for me to hear it." The song you now sing is more powerful than the economy because you have ignited your soul, and the world is staying warm around that fire. Go, and be...you!!!

About Shawn

A thought leader in the data space and on leadership, Shawn Mason helps enterprises steer towards a more accessible approach to data. He provides insightful and thought-provoking ideas on leadership and change. Those recommendations have made tremendous impact in others' lives and how they relate to others. He has a knack for recommending small tweaks that produce consistent and incremental results in processes and process management. He is currently a doctoral candidate in Strategic Leadership.

Shawn's business activities have led to a huge passion for exploring the world. He travels abroad often with his wife, and they are often joined by one or more of their children. The couple's ability to find great deals and create adventures led to a demand for how they do it. This demand led to the creation of a travel company that advises and books travel on great deals and adventures.

Shawn has extensive experience in real estate investing, rehabbing, and storage units. He often works with other investors as both silent and active partners on various deals. In his downtime, Shawn invests his time and resources to help feed orphaned children in Uganda and other countries.

You can find out more at:

- www.InvestWithShawn.com
- www.FeedTheChildrenWithShawn.com
- https://tmason.dreamvacations.com

CHAPTER 11

NIDO'S LAWS FOR MAKING YOUR WAY THE WINNING WAY

BY NICK NANTON

Your present circumstances don't determine where you go; they merely determine where you start.
~ Dr. Nido R. Qubein

Dr. Qubein's above quote is a winning way to approach your business. Qubein's philosophy has even more impact when you know his life story – he came to this country as a teenager with $50 in his pocket and is now the president of High Point University, a board member for two Fortune 500 companies, a sought-after speaker, and a published author.

So where is the starting point for you to turn your present circumstances into the winning way that Qubein created for himself? We were fortunate enough to spend time with Dr. Qubein, visiting him at HPU (High Point University) while we shot a documentary about his life. From watching him in action we garnered what we like to call 'Nido's Laws' – Qubein's approach for winning in his business endeavors, at the university, and in his consulting with others to develop the success of their businesses. What follows are our interpretations of how he has done it and how you can create that winning way for yourself.

YOUR BUSINESS WINS WHEN YOU CREATE VALUE

While he is an impressive guy in general, what blew us away was watching Dr. Qubein do a 90 minute presentation to potential freshman and their parents – consumers with hugely different needs and concerns. By the end of his speech the students were stoked about campus life, and the parents, who had come in getting ready to be bored to sleep (like they were at most university visits!) were hoping and praying that their child would have the privilege to attend the university and learn from such an inspiring leader.

How did he do it? Well, we've always said that price is only an issue when value is a mystery. If you don't create value, then you are just a commodity. High Point University (HPU) stands out because Dr. Qubein shows his target market not just what HPU is, but what it can do for each of them. President Qubein has partnered with his faculty and staff to focus on offering experiential education and holistic, values-based learning. They want graduates prepared to live a life of both success and significance. Qubein even teaches a class to all freshmen titled, 'The President's Seminar on Life Skills' where he shares the habits, skills, values, and practical intelligence that the students need to succeed in an ever-changing world.

Nido's first law is to create value. There are three ways we saw Qubein creating value in his businesses and at the school. The first is exactly what we experienced in the presentation for the potential students and their parents. By matching the vision and mission of the institution with the dynamic persona of the president, Qubein created a winning brand. Then he used that 90-minute speech to connect the parents and students to each other, to their goals, and to the vision of an HPU education. When you can create a brand that is identified with a 'celebrity' persona, you create value by connecting a person to the product.

The second way to create value is through creating a quality culture for your organization. Your company should make everyone from the CEO to the hourly worker responsible for putting value into the product. Motivate your employees to see their role as value adder rather than as the task-oriented machine operator or order processor.

Pride is a powerful motivator – everybody is proud of something! If you can find out what makes your people proud, you can use that insight to channel their motivation. As Robert W. Darvin, the founder of several winning companies, including Scandinavian Design, Inc. observes: "There's only one thing that counts in a business: building the selfesteem of your employees. Nothing else matters, because what they feel about themselves is what they give to your customers. If an employee comes to work not liking his job, not feeling good about himself, you can be sure that your customers will go away not liking or feeling good about your company."

When you have a culture of value adders, you empower everyone in your business to share the value of your product with your clients. Adding this kind of value makes your business more than a commodity – you will have a brand that clients feel connected to and trust.

YOUR CUSTOMER BASE GROWS WHEN YOU INTERPRET THE VALUE

It doesn't do you any good to offer a service unless your clients are sure of how it benefits them. At HPU there is a Ruth's Chris-style steakhouse on campus that students can use on their dining plan to eat at once a week. The immediate reaction of each parent is, "What? Is that how my money is going to be spent?" A totally reasonable response until you interpret the value – the steakhouse is a *learning lab* where students are allowed to come once a week. They must make a reservation, dress appropriately and be prepared to have an etiquette lesson. If they miss their reservation they are banned for a month! Students come away knowing how to host a client dinner or have a high level interview at a five star restaurant. Once the value is interpreted, the parents are not only onboard, they are convinced this is vital to their child's success.

This is Nido's second law – interpret the value. Qubein says, "When we admit a student to HPU, we commit our full resources to ensure their success." That is echoed in the stories of the students, like Olivia French, a junior communication major. One of the first classes she took as a freshman was a first-year seminar called "The World is Flat: Globalization of Economics." HPU students get to know their professors in the classroom because the class sizes are so small (another win for the consumer). As a journalism major with an English writing minor, an economics and any other science or math class was like a foreign language to Olivia. When she stepped into that classroom the first day and saw how small the class was, it did not seem like a win to her. In fact, panic set in. With a small, engaged classroom there was no place to hide and it would be easy for Olivia to be called on by the professor.

Dr. Suryadipta Roy not only managed to help Olivia understand globalization and economics (a feat in itself), he also managed to become one of her favorite professors during her time at HPU. Even in her junior year, she would see him on campus and he would ask how she was doing. She was amazed that he remembered not only her and her fears, but her name. To HPU's and Olivia's credit she was able to interpret the value of having a small class with an engaged professor who tailored his approach to motivate her to success. "He helped me to step outside of my comfort zone—a skill that is necessary for a journalist—and gave me the opportunity to understand concepts that I wouldn't have explored on my own."

Oprah would call Olivia's value interpretation an 'Aha Moment'. When your brand's values, and the people enacting those values align the value of your services, are interpreted for your clients—that is what enables those kinds of loyalty moments. So ask these questions – am I interpreting the value of my services from the POV of the buyer? Does our customer base understand how the value applies to them and their needs? Am I creating a win, a loyalty moment, for our clients when the value is interpreted for them?

YOUR BRAND WINS WHEN YOU CREATE A WINNING ENVIRONMENT

Michael Jordan, the great National Basketball Association superstar, showed his team spirit in the 1992 NBA playoffs when, after a stunning individual performance in which his team lost, he began feeding the ball to his teammates. Jordan's personal score fell considerably, but his team won.

Nido's third law is to create a winning environment for both your team and your clients. Qubein believes that the winning environment is created from within, by the staff first. When people in an organization compete with one another for glory, only the competition wins. When they cooperate internally, they become more competitive externally – and the entire organization wins. When you cooperate with your fellow workers, everyone is pulling for you to win. When you compete against them, they're all pulling for you to lose. In today's competitive world, nobody knows everything there is to know about the business. It's a win for your business to have a true team spirit and be able to tap into the expertise of everyone on the team.

Another way that Dr. Qubein creates a winning environment at

HPU is by insisting that the campus and the staff get rid of all irritants. The price of tuition is all inclusive at HPU. On campus parking, housing, and tuition is all included in the price. They even have a concierge where students can go and get help on everything from how to load up their passport card (there's no cash on campus) to arranging a ride to the airport. The parents use the concierge as a way to get information to their student. No one has to fill out masses of paperwork on their own – they can call the concierge. By getting rid of all irritants, Dr. Qubein increases the value by making educating the student the main job of the student. Now that 40 grand starts to look like a bargain compared to the effort and extra costs of working with a state school.

A winning organization puts it all together for the customer, which makes the price make sense. As a consumer yourself, you know those irritants like extra fees and hidden costs. How many times does a customer have to click through a website to get to the Submit page? Any extra step that makes your prospect throw up their hands and say 'forget it' – those are the irritants that you have to not just reduce, but totally eliminate. Get rid of any irritants that decrease the value of your business. The ease that comes from doing business with you enhances your brand and is a product itself.

Finally, a winning environment adds 'Wow' to the experience.

When a potential student visits HPU for the first time they drive up to the college's sign and beneath it is a digital personalized welcome with the student's name and where they are from. Wow! After the presentation by Dr. Qubein every family leaves with a 'trail of tangibles' – HPU swag including a copy of Dr. Qubein's book. Wow! How many of those other 1800 colleges in HPU's market have that kind of take away? By the end of the first HPU visit there is literally no competition. Think back to Olivia's experience in economics – adding 'Wow' to your business can be done as simply as Dr. Roy did when he lived out the brand values of the organization. That behavior created a 'Wow' for the student.

The amazing thing about adding 'Wow' is that it makes people want to be a part of it. How many students do you think stop the car to take pictures under the personalized welcome sign? Right. Every one of them. Then they Instagram, Facebook and Tweet those photos, all with a hash tag that markets High Point University. Wow.

When you add 'Wow' it needs to have a purpose. Wow for Wow's sake doesn't work. Instead, differentiate with relevance. For instance HPU is building a Center for Student Success. They aren't building this innovative, modern facility just because it's cool. They're building it because internships and career connections are most relevant to their students. Yes, taking classes and working with career counselors in a building that Google employees would envy IS different. But the customer finds true value in the fact that the facility and its programs are instrumental in preparing them for success beyond graduation. You may offer something unique to your clients, but does it really benefit them?

It's up to you, not your circumstances, to determine which way your business goes. If you are looking for the way to win then use Nido's laws – create value, interpret that value, and establish an environment of value adders who eliminate irritants and add 'Wow'. By following these laws you can create the kind of winning culture that Qubein is famous for creating everywhere he goes.

About Nick

From the slums of Port au Prince, Haiti, with special forces raiding a sex-trafficking ring and freeing children, to the Virgin Galactic Space Port in Mojave with Sir Richard Branson, the 22-Time Emmy Award Winning Director/Producer, Nick Nanton, has become known for telling stories that connect. Why? Because he focuses on the most fascinating subject in the world: PEOPLE.

As a storyteller and Best-Selling Author, Nick has shared his message with millions of people through his documentaries, speeches, blogs, lectures, and best-selling books. Nick's book *StorySelling* hit *The Wall Street Journal* Best-Seller list and is available on Audible as an audio book. Nick has directed more than 60 documentaries and a sold out Broadway Show (garnering 43 Emmy nominations in multiple regions and 22 wins), including:

- *DREAM BIG: Rudy Ruettiger LIVE on Broadway*
- *Visioneer: The Peter Diamandis Story*
- *Rudy Ruettiger: The Walk On*
- *Operation Toussaint*
- *The Rebound*

Nick has shared the stage, co-authored books, and made films featuring:

– Larry King
– Dick Vitale
– Kenny Chesney
– Charles Barkley
– Coach Mike Krzyzewski
– Jack Nicklaus
– Tony Robbins
– Steve Forbes
– will.i.am
– Sir Richard Branson
– Dean Kamen
– Ray Kurzweil
– Lisa Nichols
– Peter Diamandis
……and many more

Nick specializes in bringing the element of human connection to every viewer, no matter the subject. He is currently directing and hosting the series: *In Case You Didn't Know* (Season 1 Executive Produced by Larry King), featuring legends in the worlds of business, entrepreneurship, personal development, technology, and sports.

Printed in the USA
CPSIA information can be obtained
at www.ICGtesting.com
LVHW022125191023
761583LV00030B/381/J

9 798986 209784